# Huguenot Silver in England
## 1688-1727

# Faber Monographs on Silver

GENERAL EDITOR: A. G. GRIMWADE F.S.A.

★

HUGUENOT SILVER IN ENGLAND 1688–1727
by J. F. Hayward

(in preparation)

RESTORATION SILVER by C. C. Oman

REGENCY SILVER by Norman Penzer

ELIZABETHAN SILVER by Gerald Taylor

ADAM SILVER by Robert Rowe

SPOONS by Mrs. G. E. P. How

VICTORIAN SILVER by Mrs. Shirley Bury

ROCOCO SILVER by A. G. Grimwade

*Gold ewer and dish. Pierre Platel, 1701.*
*Engraved arms of the Dukes of Devonshire.*
*Devonshire Collections. Ewer 7 in. high. Dish 10¾ in. long.*

# HUGUENOT SILVER
# IN ENGLAND

## 1688–1727

by

J. F. HAYWARD

FABER AND FABER

24 Russell Square

London

*First published in mcmlix*
*by Faber and Faber Limited*
*24 Russell Square London W.C.1*
*Printed in Great Britain by*
*R. MacLehose and Company Limited*
*The University Press Glasgow*
*All rights reserved*

# Acknowledgements

I HAVE been greatly assisted in the preparation of this book by the invaluable advice of Mr. Charles Oman, Keeper of the Department of Metalwork in the Victoria and Albert Museum. I wish to thank Mr. Claude Blair, Assistant Keeper of the Department of Metalwork for reading the manuscript and Miss Elizabeth Murdoch for correcting the proofs, making the index and undertaking all the multifarious tasks of preparing the text for publication.

Plates, 28, 82A, 84, 85A, 85B, and 86 are reproduced by gracious permission of Her Majesty the Queen; I also have to thank the following for permission to reproduce the illustrations in this book:

The Marchioness of Cholmondeley,
E. Assheton Bennett, Esq.,
The Worshipful Company of Goldsmiths,
The Ashmolean Museum, Oxford,
The British Museum,
The Glasgow Art Gallery and Museum,
The Hermitage Museum, Leningrad,
The Metropolitan Museum, New York,
The Rikjsmuseum, Amsterdam,
The Victoria and Albert Museum,
The National Trust,
Messrs. Christie, Manson & Woods, Ltd.,
Messrs. How of Edinburgh, Ltd.,
Messrs. Thomas Lumley, Ltd.,
The Ministry of Works.

# Contents

# Illustrations

Gold ewer and dish. Devonshire Collections. Pierre Platel, 1701.

*frontispiece*

---

*at the end of the book*

[xi]

engraving attributed to William Hogarth. Victoria and
Albert Museum

# Introduction

The period covered by this book begins with a political event which had a strong influence on the history of the goldsmiths' art in England. This was the enforced abdication of the Stuart king, James II and his replacement by the Dutch prince, William of Orange. William's accession to the English throne gave great impetus to the taste for foreign, in particular French, fashions which had become increasingly apparent in the decade prior to 1688. The period ends in 1727 with the death of George I, the first Hanoverian king of England, by which time the foreign influences of the late seventeenth century had been incorporated in a new English style. Though approximate limits for this book are thus laid down, it is, in fact, more concerned with stylistic than with historical boundaries. Its main intention is to study, without excessive regard to chronological limits, the development and significance of the new style which was brought to England from France by the refugee Huguenots in the 1680's, and which within a decade had gained general acceptance amongst the main patrons of the goldsmith in this country. It was this style that created vessel forms which are now generally recognized as the most beautiful and the best adapted to their material in the whole history of English goldsmiths' work.

The late seventeenth and early eighteenth centuries saw the foundation of great fortunes by both landowners and merchants. The former were materially assisted by the Government bounty on corn and by the extension of the enclosures which made possible larger-scale and more progressive farming. Commerce frequently brought immense rewards to those who embarked upon it. At the same time as markets were expanding the foundation of the Joint Stock Companies reduced the investors' risks, and both ship-building and navigation made great progress. Much of the money thus made was invested in the purchase of land and in the building or re-building of country mansions, but what was not required for these purposes was invested in plate, which, in spite of the increasing cost of workmanship, was still regarded as a convenient method of holding ready capital. A nobleman's status was to some extent judged by the amount and quality of his plate, and a figure of some 4,000 ounces of plate was considered to be the minimum required to support the state of a British ambassador to a foreign court.

# CHAPTER I

# The Huguenot Style

The Glorious Revolution of 1688, though it brought a Dutch sovereign to the English throne, had the anomalous effect of substituting French fashion for the Dutch fashion hitherto predominant in the London goldsmiths' shops. Since the restoration of the monarchy in 1660, English goldsmiths had looked to Holland for their models and Charles II himself had given important commissions to a Dutch goldsmith. By 1688 France, under the rule of Louis XIV, was leading fashions in the applied arts throughout Western Europe, and the rather provincial forms of Baroque still practised by the goldsmiths of Holland and Flanders were already giving way to the more stately classicism of Louis XIV's Grand Manner. In spite of the incessant wars between Holland and France, Holland remained open to French influence in the arts and Louis XIV's repression of the French Protestants, culminating in the Revocation of the Edict of Nantes in 1685, eventually brought to Holland French craftsmen to work in the style that had preceded them. Many Huguenots had also come to England before 1688, but the replacement of Catholic James II by Protestant William and Mary made England a more certain refuge for them. A number of Huguenots who had gone first to Holland followed the court to England and the regular payment of the Royal Bounty funds to the more necessitous doubtless tempted others.[1] William III's own court architect and designer, Daniel Marot, was a Huguenot refugee born in Paris who had entered the service of William of Orange on the Revocation of the Edict of Nantes.[2] He

---

[1] Public appeals for funds to relieve the want of the Huguenots were made in 1681, 1686, 1688, 1694 and 1699. The money thus obtained was supplemented by payments from the Privy Purse, and from 1690 to 1702 an annual grant of £15,000 was made by Parliament. Interrupted in 1702, the grant was subsequently resumed on a lesser scale.

[2] He described himself as 'Architecte du Roy de la Grande Bretagne'.

is known to have been in England in 1695 and 1696 and again in 1698, and his version of the monumental Louis XIV style was widely spread by the large number of sheets of engraved ornament which were published after his designs.

The arrival of William thus set the seal of royal approval on the French style, which had hitherto been practised only by the small number of French Huguenot refugee goldsmiths who had been allowed to set up independently in London. After 1688 the advantage was definitely with the immigré goldsmiths and within two decades the fashion derived from Dutch sources which had persisted since the Restoration had become obsolete. Such was the predominance of the new fashion throughout Western Europe that the English goldsmiths would have been constrained to follow it even without the influx of the Huguenots to show them the way. The Huguenots were in fact particularly fortunate to arrive at a time when a change in fashion was due, and it was not long before they were securing the major orders for new plate in London.

The change-over to the new fashions and techniques was not achieved without difficulty. The native-born goldsmiths endeavoured to resist both the new methods and the immigré rivals who introduced them. The story of the efforts of the London goldsmiths' trade to exclude the Huguenots is a long one and is dealt with in Chapter II. The achievement of the latter in gaining so many and such important commissions for silver within a decade or so of their arrival in the country is nothing short of remarkable. The speed with which they achieved predominance can be attributed to a combination of favourable circumstances, perhaps reinforced, as will be seen from the terms of one of the petitions of the London goldsmiths given below (p. 20), by their willingness to accept lower rates for working plate.

The Carolean style in design and decoration of plate had been of mainly Dutch inspiration and so we find in the 1690's two Continental styles, French Huguenot and Dutch, competing for acceptance. The first of the Carolean features to be abandoned was the bold embossed floral ornament which had appeared mainly on the borders of salvers and on two-handled cups. Van Vianen-like grotesque forms and also chinoiseries, which had been amongst the most attractive decorative devices of the Carolean period, were the next to go, though the flat-chased chinoiseries survived into the late 1690's on a few pieces, mainly tankards and mugs.[1] By about 1700 Carolean ornament had completely disappeared, except on a few pieces such as the reflector plates of wall-sconces, which were particularly well adapted in design to embossed ornament. The English-born goldsmiths did not at first adopt the French style, but took over another Dutch form of ornament, the embossing of the surface with a series of parallel vertical flutes, sometimes covering the whole of it, sometimes only part. Examples are illustrated in Pls. 4, 14A and 19A, the first, strangely enough, the work of a Huguenot, presumably working to special order.

Subsequently an anglicized version of this fluted decoration was introduced: in this case the lower part only of the body was decorated with spiral gadroons and flutes set alternately, the sequence being interrupted at one point by a large symmetrical Baroque cartouche (Pl. 13B). Within this cartouche was an oval escutcheon for the coat of arms of the owner, the space between the outer scrolls and the escutcheon usually being filled with a chased or incised scale pattern. The design of the escutcheon probably went back to some mid-seventeenth-century pattern book and must have seemed curiously old-fashioned in comparison with the Huguenot designs. Two-handled cups decorated in this manner retained their popularity for a very long time, and cheap thin cups of this type were still being made during the third quarter of the eighteenth century. This same ornament was also much used on monteiths, tankards and mugs, though such pieces would hardly have satisfied the more sophisticated customer. Vessels decorated in this somewhat out-moded way were the speciality of a small number of goldsmiths, including, in particular, Seth Lofthouse.

After 1700 the French taste was generally dominant and the most important pieces of plate were either made by Huguenots or executed in a style that was derived from them. Alongside this rich Huguenot style, however, another fashion for plate of extreme sobriety arose, a reduction of the Huguenot designs to their fundamental form, free of all ornamentation. This style is sometimes claimed to be of English origin and there is no doubt that it was particularly well suited to the English artistic temperament. Such claims in favour of an English origin must be regarded with reserve

---

[1] For examples see Toronto Exhibition 1958, where the following pieces with chinoiserie ornament were shown: a covered cup of 1689 (fig. 36, no. E2), a pair of mugs of 1689 (no. E1) and a punch-bowl of 1692 (no. E10).

as similar fashions were adopted by the goldsmiths of Germany, the Low Countries and Scandinavia. There can, in any case, be no doubt that the original impetus came from France. In this style no ornament whatever was applied, and forms were based on the rectangle, the hexagon and the octagon. For his effect the goldsmith relied upon excellence of proportion and the contrasting reflections from the plain surfaces. Nearly all kinds of plate were made on an octagonal or hexagonal plan, from large bowls and dishes to small cups and saucers (Pl. 45B), and those which, by reason of their function, could not be made to octagonal shape were set on an octagonal foot and stem (Pls. 75, 76). Silver vessels of octagonal plan decorated only with stepped mouldings are commonly known as 'Queen Anne', but in fact the style remained fashionable during the reign of George I and could just as well be described as 'Early Georgian'.

Towards the end of the period the distinction between Huguenots and English-born goldsmiths became less marked; the latter had assimilated much of the Huguenot manner, and it is no longer possible to pick out a piece made by a Huguenot without looking at the maker's mark. The ornament became lighter in character; in place of the heavy plastic detail and bold relief of the earlier Huguenots who had been trained in France, we find the more delicate interlaced strapwork and trelliswork typical of the Régence style in France (Pl. 25). This strapwork was executed either by casting or by engraving, and was used by both Huguenots and English-born goldsmiths, though the productions of the former still tended to be more richly decorated. At the same time the profile of the handles of vessels became more complex, with a double scroll instead of the S-scroll of the early eighteenth-century pieces. In the mature works of the greatest of the second generation Huguenots, such as Paul de Lamerie, one finds medallions with profile heads forming the centre point of panels of foliated strapwork, which in turn are enclosed within cartouches composed of scrolls and foliage, as on the Lamerie basin or dish made for the Hon. George Treby (Pls. 62 and 63). The finest works in this style mostly date from the early years of George II's reign and do not, therefore, come within the scope of this volume. Prototypes for these later phases of Huguenot ornament can also be found in the French goldsmiths' pattern books of the early eighteenth century.

## The Huguenot Style

The Huguenot style in silver was based on the vast quantity of ornamental designs produced by three great masters of ornament who between them had created the majestic Louis XIV style. These were Paul Ducerceau (*c.* 1630–1713), Jean Berain (1637–1711) and Jean Lepautre (1618–82).[1] The decorative style evolved by these masters was in turn translated into terms more suitable for goldsmiths' use by lesser masters such as M.P. Mouton of Lyons who published a *Livre de desseins pour toute sorte d'ouvrages d'orfèvrerie,* and by Masson, whose *Nouveaux desseins pour graver sur l'orfèvrerie* published in Paris by Mariette, show French late Baroque ornament at its richest. While the Huguenots had, therefore, a mass of published material to which they might turn for inspiration or example, the English goldsmiths still relied on designs and traditions that had never been permanently recorded on paper.

The changes that took place in silver design at this time led to innovations not only in vessel form but also in technique of manufacture and constituted eventually a decisive break with tradition. The Carolean style had, with few exceptions, called for lavish embossed ornament; in order to execute this embossed ornament, it was necessary to work in metal sufficiently thin to be stretched without excessive labour to the shapes required by the design.

The Carolean floral patterns, though effective at a distance, were often lacking in proportion and in solidity, giving an impression that the metal had been skimped in order to achieve the maximum effect at the minimum cost in precious metal. Embossed ornament could not be executed on very narrow surfaces and certain parts, such as handles of cups or bracket ornaments to stems, had always been cast. It was in the production of these small cast details that the weakness of the pre-Huguenot goldsmiths is revealed, for they were often left rough from the casting or at best but carelessly finished. The French style with its heavy mouldings and its ornament cast in high relief called for different techniques of manufacture and the familiarity of the Huguenot goldsmiths with these techniques doubtless gave them a considerable advantage over their English-born competitors. The new style involved a far more

---

[1] While their works covered a far wider field than that of goldsmiths' work alone, Jean Berain produced a number of drawings with designs for silver, and Jean Lepautre included amongst his vast œuvre of over 2,200 etchings a set of designs for silver andirons.

extravagant use of silver. Whereas formerly the ornament had been worked in the walls of the vessel, which were of uniform thickness throughout, now the ornament, cast separately and applied, added greatly to the weight. Not all the ornament was cast. Vessels were still raised on the stake and ornament such as gadrooning or fluting was still hammered out of the body, but the straps and leaves which are so characteristic a feature of the ornament of this time were cast separately and applied.

The so-called cut-card work was another important feature of Huguenot decoration, but it was introduced to England long before the Huguenots arrived. It appears as early as 1667 on a pair of small covered cups in the Ashmolean Museum, Oxford. At first, it had consisted of applying by soldering cut-out, usually foliate, patterns in flat sheet to plain surfaces such as the cover of a cup or the underside of a porringer or salver. It was further developed by being applied in separate leaves instead of one single sheet, and also, towards the end of the seventeenth century, by using it in more than one layer (Pl. 29), sometimes with a central rib or moulding set over a double thickness of cut sheet (Pl. 34B). This called for considerable skill in the use of solders flowing at different temperatures.

Perhaps the most imposing feature of the new style was the imaginative use of plastic decoration. There seems to be no doubt that the ability to produce sculptural forms of great majesty was a Huguenot achievement. We find in their ornament a host of sculptural details, finely modelled caryatid handles, bold masks, rich mouldings and florid acanthus foliage, all basic features of the French Louis XIV style, both in furniture and in plate. The earlier English plastic ornament based on Dutch Baroque lobate forms or composed of naturalistic flower motifs had been strongly anti-classical in character. The classical Baroque of the new style swept away such provincial trends in ornament in England as it did throughout Western Europe.

The features of late seventeenth and early eighteenth-century silver that are now most admired are its sobriety, combined with elegance of form, and the restrained character of its ornament, which never obscures or interferes with its function. These characteristics were not by any means the exclusive property of the Huguenot goldsmiths. It would, indeed, be an over-simplification to think that all silver made before 1688 was invariably lavishly embossed. Certain types of object had long been produced in simple forms, some almost exclusively so. Amongst the latter may be mentioned the tankard, the barrel of which was either left plain, flat-chased with chinoiseries or, at the most, decorated with a wreath around the lower half. Plain designs, often combined with the use of an octagonal section, were coming into fashion and would eventually have become established in England without the intervention of the Huguenot immigrés.

One must avoid attributing to the Huguenots a greater influence on English style than they actually exercised. The two styles existed side by side for nearly a generation before they merged into one. The English goldsmiths persisted with their plain style, relying for effect upon surface quality and excellence of proportion, while the Huguenots enriched their work with cast or engraved ornament, which, though perhaps less rich than would have been considered suitable for a wealthy French patron, conferred a dignity and distinction to their pieces that was absent in the more modest English productions. The Huguenots for their part were perfectly capable of producing the plainer pieces, which in any case required less labour to make, but it is doubtful whether, at any rate in the early stages, the average English-born goldsmith could have turned out work to equal the more extravagant Huguenot pieces.

From the time of their first arrival in England we find pieces of silver of extremely sober design bearing the makers' marks of Huguenot goldsmiths. It is probable that such concessions to English taste for simplicity were made at the wish of the patron whose taste was the ultimate factor in determining design in eighteenth-century silver. While the Huguenot goldsmith preferred to decorate his wares, he was doubtless prepared and, indeed, constrained in the earlier years of his career to accept orders from the more sober patrons who preferred silver of simple design or the less moneyed ones who could not afford plate of elaborate fashion. The famous Huguenot goldsmith, Paul de Lamerie, is a case in point. The earliest recorded piece by Lamerie dates from 1711/12, but it was not until he had been working as an independent goldsmith for eight years that we find him producing really elaborate pieces in what is usually described as the Huguenot style, as for example the wine-cooler he made for the Duke of Sutherland[1] in 1719. Eventually he obtained numerous

[1] Ill., P. A. S. Phillips, *Paul de Lamerie*, Pl. VIII.

commissions for elaborately-worked plate and created some of the richest pieces produced in this country (see Pls. 8, 24, 62 and 63). To the end of his working life, however, he continued to produce a limited amount of undecorated plate.

Just as some of the Huguenot makers worked from time to time in the plain English manner, so we find a small group of English-born makers who successfully adopted the grand manner of the Huguenots. Foremost amongst them are the brothers, George and Francis Garthorne (Pls. 28, 77 and 80A) and Benjamin Pyne (Pls. 1, 38). Whether these goldsmiths employed Huguenot journeymen or did in fact master the new style themselves is a problem that we cannot at present solve.

French customs of eating and drinking differed in some respects from those current in England and we find these differences reflected in some of the Huguenot productions. The range of English silver was certainly enriched by the Huguenots for they introduced into this country the tall helmet-shaped ewer (Pls. 34A, B) with shaped basin en suite, the pilgrim bottle (Pl. 29), the soup tureen (Pl. 65A) and the écuelle, a flat covered bowl with two flat ear-like handles (Pl. 69A, B). This last piece never seems to have become so popular in this country as it was on the Continent, where it was the standard present made to a wife in childbed. On the other hand, beer-tankards, which were made in such large numbers by the English goldsmiths, were not used in France and few were made by Huguenots over here. The silver coffee-beaker, a small beaker with slightly everted sides standing on a low foot, which was very common in France, never came to England, presumably because the English preferred to use oriental porcelain or Dutch earthenware (Pl. 47). In view of its heat-conducting qualities, silver was in fact far from suitable for coffee or teacups. The latter were indeed known in England (Pl. 45B), but were soon given up in favour of a material that did not conduct heat so readily.

Owing to the extremely radical destruction of French silver ordered by Louis XIV to provide bullion to pay for the French wars, very little silver of the period immediately preceding or following the Revocation of the Edict of Nantes survives. It is, therefore, hardly possible to make a comparison between the plate made by Huguenot craftsmen in England and that made by their contemporaries in France. One source that is available is the series of pattern books issued for the guidance of French silversmiths at this epoch. To judge by the few surviving pieces of French Louis XIV silver and by these pattern books,[1] it would seem that the Huguenots adopted in England a style considerably more restrained than that current amongst fashionable Parisian goldsmiths. This may well be so, but it must not be forgotten that pattern books as a whole often fail to take into account considerations of cost of the object designed or the practical problems of making it. As a whole it may be said that the surviving articles of a period tend to be rather less elaborate than the designs in the contemporary pattern books lead one to expect.

One circumstance remains to be mentioned that throws some light on the development of the Huguenot goldsmiths in London. This is the fact that they came not from Paris but from the French Provinces. By a fortunate chance the names of the towns of origin of most of the Huguenots are known from the records of the distribution of the Royal Bounty funds.[2] The payments from this fund, which was established in order to provide assistance for needy Huguenots and was administered by the Huguenots themselves, frequently give the town of origin of the recipient of relief. The payments were mostly made to elderly persons or widows, and the individuals whose names appear were not, therefore, goldsmiths but their parents or elderly relatives. Nevertheless, the family names enable us to establish the origin of a great many of the leading Huguenot goldsmiths. In the 1687 lists we already find the family names of many of the best-known goldsmiths, including Archambo, Mettayer, Crespin, Margas, Le Sage, Liger and Pilleau. By 1690 we find both Vincent and Chartier as well. The town of origin of these families is not known in every case, but we know that Archambo came from the Isle d'Oléron, Mettayer from Poitou, Harache and Margas from Rouen, Le Sage from Alençon, Liger from Saumur, Platel from Lorraine and Pilleau from the province of Maine. From other sources we know that David Willaume, who was one of the most productive of all the immigré goldsmiths in London, came from Metz. Some of these goldsmiths came over to England as boys and had never actually worked in France. They were, however, apprenticed to Huguenot

---

[1] For reproductions of designs from French goldsmiths' pattern books see *Œuvres de Bijouterie et Joaillerie des XVIIe et XVIIIe Siècles.*

[2] A list of payments to Huguenot goldsmiths or their dependants, collected by Mr. P. A. S. Phillips, is in the library of the Worshipful Company of Goldsmiths.

goldsmiths over here and the French character of their work persisted in spite of their having been trained in England. Among the later generation who had learnt their trade in part or entirely in England were Louis Mettayer who registered his mark in 1700, Jean Liger in 1703, Jacob Margas in 1706, John Le Sage in 1708 and James Fraillon in 1710. Among those who had served an apprenticeship in England were Louis Mettayer, apprenticed to David Willaume; Paul de Lamerie, apprenticed to Pierre Platel; and Augustine Courtauld, apprenticed to Simon Pantin. A third generation of Huguenot goldsmiths who had been born in England did not enter their marks until the 1720's. By this time the Huguenot and the native English styles had coalesced, though there is no doubt that the Huguenot characteristics were predominant.

While the nobility and gentry gave large commissions to the Huguenots, the royal family gave the lion's share of their orders to English-born goldsmiths. So little of the English royal plate of the late seventeenth and early eighteenth centuries has survived that it is difficult to make any definite statements about its original composition, but William III's main orders went at first to Charles Shelley, who had supplied plate to Charles II, and subsequently to the brothers, Francis and George Garthorne. The Garthornes, however, adopted wholeheartedly the French style. The superb ewer of 1690 by Francis Garthorne amongst the royal plate[1] has already such French features as a harp-shaped handle, a spout with floral enrichment and cut-card ornament in two layers. From the Lord Chamberlain's accounts, we know that William III also patronized the Huguenot, Philip Rollos, and the Cumberland plate, now belonging to the Duke of Brunswick but formerly part of the English royal plate, includes a gold salver of 1691 by Pierre Harache, engraved with the cipher of William III.

Queen Anne employed the Garthornes and subsequently, Anthony Nelme and Benjamin Pyne. Amongst the Cumberland plate there was also a basin and ewer with the royal arms of Queen Anne by David Willaume with the London hall-mark for 1702.

During George I's reign the officials responsible for ordering plate spread their commissions more widely. Amongst makers of surviving pieces, either in the royal plate or in the Cumberland collection, Philip Rollos, Samuel Margas, James Fraillon and

---

[1] Ill., E. A. Jones, *Windsor Castle Plate*, Pl. XXI.

Anne Tanqueray, all Huguenots, are represented. Furthermore, a large order for a complete service of plate for the use of George, Prince of Wales, later George II, went to Pierre Platel early in George I's reign. This service, which is engraved with the Prince of Wales's badge and initials G.P. was sent over to Hanover, a circumstance which saved it from the melting pot to which most of the English early eighteenth-century royal plate was consigned by George IV when he was building up the so-called Grand Service. The Platel service remained at Hanover until after the First World War, when it was sold in London and dispersed.

Amongst the important commissions secured by the Huguenot goldsmiths was that for the provision of a large service for the Empress Catherine of Russia, comprising in 1734 36 pieces of gilt plate and 329 of white. What little of this service now remains is in the Hermitage; most of it was melted subsequently. Judging by the remaining pieces, which are far from uniform in design or ornament, it would seem that the service must have been brought together by purchasing pieces which the various Huguenot goldsmiths had in stock. Each was then engraved with the Russian imperial arms. The service consists now of a cup and cover by Paul Crespin, two pairs of jugs by Anne Tanqueray, a soup tureen by Simon Pantin (Pl. 65A), a basin and ewer by Samuel Margas, three mugs by William Fleming and a pair of dishes without marks. A number of the pieces bear only the maker's mark and have not been submitted for assay at Goldsmiths' Hall; amongst them the largest pieces: namely the basin and ewer and the tureen. As the service was ordered for a foreign customer and would not be offered for sale in this country, it was probably thought that the formality of assay might safely be dispensed with and the heavy plate tax of 6d. per ounce thereby avoided. Those pieces belonging to the service which are marked bear the London hall-mark for 1725/6; it is surprising to find that forty years after the first Huguenot goldsmiths had started work in London, their successors should still have kept distinct from the native goldsmiths. By this time there was no longer any great distinction in style between Huguenot and non-Huguenot productions, but the fact that the whole of what must have been an important order went to Huguenots shows that they must have been in close touch with each other.

In spite of their success in gaining important orders, the Huguenots do not seem to have acquired great fortunes. At all events the names of relatives of nearly all the prominent Huguenot gold-smiths appear on the lists of necessitous persons in receipt of charity from the Royal Bounty funds. The most striking exception is David Willaume, who eventually became Lord of the Manor of Tingrith in Bedfordshire, where his family, named Tanqueray-Willaume through marriage with the goldsmith family of that name, survived into the present century. His son, David Willaume, junior, who entered his mark in 1720, is recorded as having kept running cashes at the Sign of the Golden Ball in St. James's Street; that is to say, he operated as a banker as well as a goldsmith.

CHAPTER II

# The Huguenot Goldsmiths in England

---

As has already been indicated, the most important single
event in the period covered by this book was the arrival of
the Huguenot goldsmiths from France, bringing with
them a style which was hardly known in this country. The impact
of this new style and the new methods of manufacture that it
called for exercised so decisive an influence on English gold-
smithing that some account of the historical events which preceded
and followed upon the Huguenot migration is indispensable.

The position of the Huguenot inhabitants of France had been
governed since 1598 by the Edict of Nantes which had marked the
end of the French Wars of Religion. This Edict granted to the
Huguenots the right to worship according to their own ritual, to
write in defence of their own doctrines and to hold both military
and civil appointments. The seventeenth century had seen a somewhat uneasy truce between the two religions in France, broken by
more than one revolt, but the terms of the Edict were confirmed
from time to time and were regarded as fundamental guarantees of
the status of the Huguenots. The political climate became very
different for the Huguenots during the reign of Louis XIV,
although his accession to the throne in 1643 had been accompanied
by a re-affirmation of the Edict. Louis XIV was opposed not only
to the reformed religion as such, but also to the republican ten-
dencies that were a feature of the Calvinist doctrines of the
Huguenots. As soon as his minority came to an end, he began to
curtail their privileges. The education of Huguenot children was
restricted, property bequeathed to their churches was confiscated
and a number of their churches were closed. The most disagree-
able of the measures to which he had recourse were the so-called
Dragonnades; that is, the quartering of Dragoons[1] in those towns

---

[1] The 'Dragonnades' constituted what must surely be the most anomalous

c　　　　　　　　　　　[13]

in which the Huguenot communities were most numerous. This measure was introduced in 1683 and it was in that year that the rate of emigration of Huguenots from France began to rise steeply. In 1685 the Edict of Nantes as a whole was revoked; it has been estimated that as a result of this measure some 50,000 families left France and that within a few years the total loss amounted to some 400,000 inhabitants.

The immigration of skilled workmen was regarded with mixed feelings in England and, while the more enlightened and educated were sympathetic, members of the trade guilds in London viewed this new source of competition with undisguised alarm. A contemporary account of the persecution of the French Protestants is to be found in an entry in John Evelyn's diary of 3rd November 1685:[1] 'The French persecution of the Protestants raging with the utmost barbarity, exceeded even what the very heathens used: innumerable persons of the greatest birth and riches leaving all their earthly substance, and hardly escaping with their lives, dispersed through all the countries of Europe. . . . In Holland, Denmark and all about Germany, were dispersed some hundred thousands; besides those in England, where, though multitudes of all degree sought for shelter and welcome as distressed Christians and Confessors, they found least encouragement, by a fatality of the times we were fallen into, and the uncharitable indifference of such as should have embraced them; and I pray it be not laid to our charge.' The attitude described by Evelyn can be followed in the numerous attempts made by the Goldsmiths' Company, along with other City Companies, to prevent the Huguenots from practising their trade in London. The first reference to Huguenot goldsmiths in the Minute Books of the Company is in July 1678. Under the conditions then existing, the London guilds could, by refusing to grant foreigners admission to the freedom, prevent them from exercising their trade independently except in certain restricted areas of the City which, with doubtful justice, claimed exemption from the control of the guilds. Accordingly, in 1678,

method ever of securing conversions to Christianity. The dragoons, who were recognized as the most undisciplined of the troops in the French army, were given licence to behave in the most brutal manner to the Huguenots in whose houses they were lodged. Property was stolen, women were violated and the men beaten. Their behaviour had the effect of securing very large numbers of spurious conversions.

[1] *The Diary and Correspondence of John Evelyn*, ed. W. Bray, London n.d., p. 444.

when the earliest groups of refugees were arriving, a Bill was moved in Parliament to enable foreign Protestants to exercise their trades in certain places and to enter on the usual seven years' apprenticeship.

Though few, if any, Huguenot goldsmiths had arrived at this date, we find the following entry in the minutes of the Court held at Goldsmiths' Hall on 10th July 1678: 'At this Court Sir John Shuter declared that he was desired by the Lord Mayor to acquaint the Company that there was a bill depending in Parliament for the licensing of Protestant Strangers to come from parts beyond the seas and here to exercise manual occupations without any let or molestation which if granted would very much tend to the prejudice of the natives of this kingdom and in especial to the artificers of this Company as he conceived, And therefore advised that this Court would cause some enquiry to be made in what posture that affair stood, intimating that he had heard the Corporation of Weavers and some other Companies Handicrafts men did oppose the passing of the said Bill. Whereupon the Court returned Sir John Shuter their thanks and declared it a business of great concernment to the Artificers of this Company and to be opposed by this Court on behalf of the Members in general.'[1] The proposed Bill did not become law, but the worst fears of the Goldsmiths' Company were realized when on 28th July 1681, Charles II made an order granting 'Letters of Denization under the Great Seal without any further charge whatsoever, and likewise such further privileges and immunities as are consistent with the laws for the liberty and free exercise of their trades and handicrafts'.

It is not, in fact, surprising that the less successful London goldsmiths should have been so sensitive to the effect upon their livelihood of the foreign competitors. The main advantage enjoyed by the latter was that they could offer fashions that were as yet unknown or only beginning to become known in England, and they tended, therefore, to obtain important commissions from those rich patrons who attached great significance to keeping up with the latest fashions. Foreign artists and craftsmen often succeeded in obtaining positions at Court, as the King alone could, by granting a

---

[1] Most of the extracts from the Minutes of the Goldsmiths' Company given in this chapter are printed in abbreviated form by W. S. Prideaux in *Memorials of the Goldsmith's Company*. I have, in all cases, transcribed them from the original manuscript entries in the Minute Books.

royal appointment, free an alien from the obligation to serve a seven years' apprenticeship and to become a freeman of the appropriate city guild. A foreigner, John Cooqūs,[1] had obtained some of Charles II's major commissions, including the huge silver bed of Nell Gwynne, and even as early as 1664 a petition against an Order in Council of Charles II, requiring the Company to assay and touch plate made by two Dutchmen, was addressed to the Court of the Company. According to the ancient Charter of the Goldsmiths' Company, only freemen of the Company were entitled to have their work assayed at Goldsmiths' Hall and touched with the Company's mark if the metal of which it was made reached the necessary standard of fineness. Unmarked silver could not be sold within the precincts of the city, and the Wardens of the Company had the right of search within the workshops of all goldsmiths to ensure that no pieces were made of sub-standard silver. In order, therefore, to gain a livelihood, an immigrant goldsmith had, unless he could obtain royal protection, either to work as an employee of a London goldsmith or to induce the Goldsmiths' Company to mark his wares. Though the terms of the Order of 1681 provided that the Protestant immigrés should enjoy 'such further privileges and immunities as are consistent with the laws for the liberty and free exercise of their trades and handicrafts', the Goldsmiths' Company, by refusing to assay the pieces made by foreigners, could and sometimes did render these provisions nugatory.

We find, therefore, a series of attempts on the part of Huguenot goldsmiths to get their work admitted for assay. The first reference in the Minute Books dates from 7th March 1682: 'Mr. John Dubois, merchant, requests assay and touch for an unnamed French Protestant, also recommended by the Rt. Hon. the Ld. Mayor and the Ld. Bishop of London by a paper under their hands and seals.' In spite of the considerable backing enjoyed by this applicant, the Court referred this request for further consideration.

The first Huguenot goldsmith to gain admittance to the Company was Pierre Harache, incidentally one of the most gifted amongst them. At the Court held on 21st July 1682, an Order of the Lord Mayor and Council of Aldermen of the City of London was read, requiring 'that the said Peter Harache shall be admitted into the freedom of this City by Redemption into the Company of

[1] *Antiquaries Journal*, July 1934, P. A. S. Phillips, 'John Cooqūs, Silversmith', p. 282.

Goldsmiths paying to Mr. Chamberlain to the City's use forty six shillings and eightpence'. At the same time the following certificate was presented: 'These are to certify all whom it may concern that Peter Harache, lately come from France for to avoid persecution and live quietly, is not only a Protestant, but by his Majesty's bounty is made a free denizen, that he may settle here freely with his family in token whereof we have given him this certificate.' The certificate bears five signatures including that of the minister of the French Church of the Savoy. Harache was accordingly made a freeman on payment of a fee of ten pounds. On 27th July, one week later, the Lord Mayor and Court of Aldermen made a similar order in respect of another Huguenot goldsmith, John Louis.

These two admissions had the expected repercussions at the Court of 2nd September 1682 when a petition was presented 'by John Sutton and Samuel Layfield of the Livery and one William Badcock a Cutler working in Gold and Silver on the behalf of themselves and several others free men of this city working in that Manufacture, the Content whereof was a complaint that divers aliens and Foreigners were come into this Kingdom and reside in and about this city and some made free thereof and of this Company, desiring to be relieved against such as intrude upon them and did also pray the Company would espouse their prosecutions of them'. The reply of the Court pointed out that 'they had admitted no more than two persons and these by two orders of the Lord Mayor and Court of Aldermen and that if any more should be charged upon them in that kind they would make their application to My Lord Mayor and Court of Aldermen in their behalf and endeavour as much as in them lay to remove the present grievance'. The grievance was not, however, remedied, for at the Court of 10th April of the following year two members of the Livery, Abraham Brind and John Nicholls, presented a further petition in the name of the working goldsmiths of the City 'complaining against the great numbers of alien goldsmiths that are permitted to work in and about London, of the unlimited [number] of Journeymen foreigners they keep to the undoing and impoverishing of the freemen of the Company, which to prevent the petitioners humbly pray this Court would present a petition to the Rt. Hon. the Lord Mayor and Court of Aldermen on their behalf whereby they may be relieved against so great and growing a mischief'. The Court resolved accordingly to forward their members' petition to the Lord Mayor with a further petition of their own annexed to it.

In spite of the Lord Mayor's order of 27th July 1682 requiring that John Louis should be admitted to the Goldsmiths' Company by redemption, it appears that he was not immediately admitted, for in February 1683 his case came up again before the Court of Aldermen and the Court of the Goldsmiths' Company was requested to admit him without delay or appear to give their reasons for failing to do so. The final chapter in this story is related in the Minutes of the Court of 11th November 1683, when the Wardens announced that they had been at Fulham Palace to inform the Bishop of London of 'the inconvenience that did attend the nation and more particularly this city by admitting aliens to be made free which when they have obtained do employ and set aliens to work although there be above 800 able and substantial working goldsmiths . . . besides several that cannot get a days' work in a week to maintain themselves and families who in the meantime are ready to starve'. They did not, however, succeed in converting the Bishop to their way of thinking and obtained from him only an undertaking not to make a similar request of them again. Accordingly John Louis was at last admitted to the freedom on the payment of a fine of ten pounds.

After the affair of John Louis, the Minutes of the Goldsmiths' Company contain no further references to the Huguenots for some years. There can be little doubt that the reference made in one of the petitions to the 'great numbers of alien goldsmiths' was grossly exaggerated. After the first two, who must have arrived in 1681 or early in 1682, no further Huguenot goldsmiths appear to have taken out denization papers until December 1687, when they were granted to Jean Harache, evidently a relative of Pierre Harache, Daniel Garnier and David Willaume.

There seems to have been a curious lack of consistence in the attitude of the Goldsmiths' Company to some of these Huguenot goldsmiths, since we find them allowing the latter to enter their marks at the Hall within a short time of their taking out denization papers, while they continued to raise objections to admitting them to the freedom. A typical example of this anomaly is the case of Daniel Garnier, who became a denizen in 1687, registered his mark at the Hall in 1691, but was not admitted to the freedom until 1696, and then only by order of the Lord Mayor and Court of

Aldermen. David Willaume was better treated since his mark was registered within a year of his becoming a denizen, and he was admitted to the freedom in 1693. Philip Rollos on the other hand required an order of the Lord Mayor to get him admitted on 11th August 1697.

The question arises as to how those alien goldsmiths who were refused the right of assay and touch were able to earn a living. A number were doubtless content to serve as journeymen in the workshops of English-born goldsmiths. It appears that others took up residence in what was known as the Liberty of Blackfriars; that is, in the precincts of the former monastery of Blackfriars. When the religious houses had been dissolved at the Reformation, the lay persons who came to inhabit the former monastic buildings laid claim to the privileges and legal exemptions that had once been enjoyed by the religious foundation. Even as late as the end of the seventeenth century, these long obsolete privileges were still subject to dispute, and in October 1689 a petition was presented to the Court of Aldermen of the City from the inhabitants of Blackfriars protesting against 'the late persecution of them for exercising their Trades in the said Place not being Freemen of this City'. In her study[1] of the Huguenot goldsmiths, Dr. Joan Evans gives the following account of a subsequent dispute in which a Huguenot goldsmith was concerned: 'In February 1697 there was a complaint to the Court of Aldermen by a goldsmith, Methuselah Smith, that "one George Beachlew a Foreigner and Alien works in his trade in Blackfriars pretending that it is privileged from the jurisdiction of this city". It was ordered that he should be prosecuted and that a committee should enquire into the whole question. In July 1698 this committee reported that Blackfriars was within the City's jurisdiction and that none but Freemen should trade there.' Though aliens who were not free of any Company were thereby excluded from setting up shop within the precincts of the City of London, they could, of course, always do so in the rapidly growing parts of London outside the western boundaries of the City.

Another method which was tried by the Huguenots and, in due course, noticed unfavourably by the London goldsmiths, was the old device of inducing a freeman of the Company, doubtless for a consideration, to take in their work with his own to the Hall for assay and touch. This practice was referred to in a petition pre-

[1]*Huguenot Goldsmiths in England and Ireland.*

sented to the Court of the Goldsmiths' Company on 11th August 1697. This 'humble petition' is interesting because it is signed by some of the most prominent working goldsmiths of their time, including Benjamin Pyne, Anthony Nelme, George and Francis Garthorne, Robert Timbrell and Nathaniel Locke together with 'other members of several branches of the Mistery of Goldsmiths'. The petition stated various causes that 'will in all probability lead to the beggary and impoverishment of your petitioners', amongst them the practice of certain goldsmiths of using great quantities of solder 'to great detriment of the public and discredit of English workmen in general'. A second grievance was that certain freemen had promised to have the work of aliens and foreigners 'touched at the Hall contrary to certain By-laws in the case provided'. The second abuse was not, however, checked, for in 1703 another petition to the Court thanks it for forbidding a member to bring a foreigner's goods to the Hall for assay and touch and also warns it that 'there are several Frenchmen, not free of this City, who are now endeavouring to get their freedom of the same by redemption'. This last warning had singularly little effect, for at the Court of 17th May in the following year we find aliens being admitted to the freedom upon presentation of proof of naturalization.

The final chapter in the long story of the efforts of the London goldsmiths to restrict or suppress Huguenot competition dates from 1711 when a petition was submitted to the Court by 'several working Goldsmiths'. It was actually signed by 53, including such well-known makers as William and John Fawdery, Gabriel Sleath, William Charnelhouse, John Boddington, etc. The immediate cause of the petition was the decision to prosecute a member of the Company for loading his work with excessive quantities of solder. The petition stated that 'partly by the general decay of trade and other ways by the intrusion of foreigners, several of the workmen of the said Company have for the support of their families been put under the force of underworking each other to the perfect beggary of the trade and at length under the necessity of loading their work with unnecessary qualities of solder to the wrong and prejudice of the buyer and the great discredit of the English workmen . . . that by the admittance of necessitous strangers, whose desperate fortunes obliged them to work at miserable rates, the representing members have been forced to bestow much more time and labour in working up their plate than hath been the practice of former times, when prices of workmanship were greater'. The petitioners no longer asked that the Huguenots should be excluded from the Company, since evidently too large a number had now been admitted to the freedom, but requested only that the price of plate should be advanced. At this time the goldsmith charged for plate supplied at so much an ounce for weight of silver used, plus an additional charge for fashion, that is, for working up the metal into the objects required, and it is presumably to the latter figure that the petitioners referred when they asked for an increase in the price of plate. The somewhat disingenuous terms of the petition tell us much about the consequences of the attempts of the Company to keep the Huguenot immigrants out of business. In order to compete in the disadvantageous circumstances that had been forced upon them, they had improved the standard of workmanship without asking for higher prices. In fact, these higher standards of workmanship were an inevitable consequence of the new fashion which substituted cast for embossed work. In any case, the London-born goldsmiths found themselves forced to accept these new standards of finish or lose their business to the Huguenots.

In spite of the terms of their charter, and in spite of the firm line taken by the Goldsmiths' Company towards aliens, it seems that the Company was not in fact legally entitled to withhold assay and touch from workers who were not free of the Company. In 1725 a number of workmen presented a Remonstrance to the Court of the Company, protesting, amongst other grievances, against the practice of admitting to the benefit of assay and touch those who were not freemen of the Company. The Remonstrance claimed that the law of William III (of 1697) supported their claim that only plate of freemen of the Company should be assayed and touched. The reply of the Court is particularly interesting in view of the measures that had been taken earlier to prevent the Huguenot goldsmiths from getting their silver assayed. It was to the effect that the Act of William III had provided only that no plate should be wrought or sold before being marked at Goldsmiths' Hall: further that the Attorney-General in a report to the Treasury had affirmed that the Company could not refuse to mark plate brought in by those who were not free of the Company. This opinion had, moreover, been confirmed by all the counsel consulted by the

Company on this particular point. That the assay and touch were, in fact, allowed to non-freemen is shown by the mark registration books, where we find members of various Companies, including the Drapers, Lorimers and Clock makers, registering marks. The well-known Huguenot goldsmith, Peter Archambo, was for instance, a freeman of the Butchers' Company.

# CHAPTER III

# Goldsmiths and the Hall-mark

The purpose of most art-historical study has been either to
investigate the personality of an artist or craftsman with a
view to determining the extent to which his idiosyncrasies
are reflected in his works, or to examine a group of works of art in
order to discover common features which may make possible their
attribution to a single master or a school. In the case of silver
vessels there are usually no problems of attribution. In most cases
there is a maker's mark to tell us who made a given piece, and,
with regard to silver made after 1697 we are nearly always able to
discover the name of the maker from the records of the Worshipful
Company of Goldsmiths. It was not, however, the aim of the goldsmith to achieve any particular individuality of style. He sought
rather to reproduce the manner of the most skilled amongst his
contemporaries. The uniformity of style amongst different masters
was perpetuated by the system of relying on printed pattern
books, which circulated amongst the members of the trade, as a
source of models and ideas. It is true that the English goldsmith
was less tied to pattern books than his Continental contemporary.
Whereas a number of French pattern books for goldsmiths exist
which supply designs for vessels and their decoration, the few that
appeared in England at this time are concerned only with engraved
ornament. On the other hand, one can say that certain goldsmiths
were in advance of the majority either in adopting or in developing
new styles. Amongst these are David Willaume, the maker of the
two-handled cup in Pl. 7, which, though made in 1705, anticipates
the standard type of some twenty years later, and, of course, Paul
de Lamerie, whose most striking innovations lie, however, beyond
the period covered by this book.

The choice of design did not, however, lie in the final resort
with the goldsmith at all, but with his client. Owing to the high

cost of the material, plate was for the most part made to order and not sold from stock. When placing his order, the customer was, presumably, shown patterns and chose the design which he found most pleasing. The fact that a goldsmith such as Paul de Lamerie should produce simple pieces at the same time as very richly worked plate can doubtless be explained by the need to meet the clients' taste.

Silver vessels were in most cases produced not by one man working alone, but by a workshop. The mark we find struck on a piece of silver is that of the master of the workshop, who may not have been either the maker or the retailer of the object in question. A goldsmith normally worked as a journeyman for a longer or shorter period, according to his economic circumstances, before he set up as an independent master. It follows that some pieces bearing the mark of a certain goldsmith may, in fact, have been made by another and more distinguished one before he was established on his own. In the same way, many of the Huguenots must have worked for London-born goldsmiths, while others, as we have seen above (p. 20), induced London-born goldsmiths to take in their pieces for assay and touch when Goldsmiths' Hall refused to mark pieces made by Huguenots. From all this it will be seen that the presence of a particular maker's mark is not absolute proof that the piece was made by the goldsmith to whom that mark belonged.

Another circumstance that seems at first sight surprising is the fact that handles or other plastic details apparently cast from the same mould are found on vessels bearing differing goldsmiths' marks. Some goldsmiths no doubt made the models in their own workshops, from which such details as caryatid handles or grotesque mask spouts were cast. Others, however, obtained them from a specialized model or pattern-maker, who did not, of course, hesitate to supply different goldsmiths with the same pattern. An example of the use of the same mould by different goldsmiths can be seen in the wall-sconce of 1702 by John Fawdery (Pl. 71(b)); this has been cast from the same mould as the pair of wall-sconces of 1703 by John Rand in the Victoria and Albert Museum. Again, when a large service of plate was required in a hurry, the retailer would put out the work to a number of goldsmiths who would collaborate in its production. In this case the models for the cast details might be passed from hand to hand, so that different makers' marks would be found on pieces from the same service made apparently with the same moulds.

The quantity of orders for new plate received by the goldsmiths after the accession of William and Mary was such that there was no longer enough bullion available in the trade to meet them. As the sterling standard for silver was the same as that for coin of the realm, metal for making new plate was found by melting coin, or, worse still, by clipping coins in circulation. As the disappearance from circulation of coinage was damaging to the economy of the country, it was necessary to devise some means of discouraging goldsmiths from melting coinage of the realm, and, if possible, to reverse the trend by inducing owners of plate to bring it in for conversion to coinage. Accordingly, on 25th March 1697, the Act for encouraging the bringing in of wrought plate to be coined came into force, and it was enacted that after this date 'no goldsmith, silversmith, or other person whatsoever, shall work or make or cause to be wrought or made any silver vessel or manufacture of silver, less in fineness than that of 11 oz. 10 dwt. of fine silver in every pound Troy'. The effect of this act was to render wrought plate 8 dwt. in the pound Troy finer than the sterling standard of coinage. Though the Act may have had some effect in discouraging the production of very large pieces of plate, it seems unlikely that its declared aim of persuading owners to have their plate melted was achieved. We do, however, learn from Celia Fiennes[1] that when, in 1698, she visited the Earl of Chesterfield's house at Bretby she found most of the silver had gone. . . . 'I was in severall bedchambers, one had a crimson damaske bed, the other crimson velvet set upon halfe paces, this best was the bride chamber which used to be call'd the Silver roome where the stands table and fire utensills were all massy silver, but when plaite was in nomination to pay a tax, the Earle of Chesterfield sold it all and the plaite of the house, so that when the table was spread I saw only spoones salts and forkes and the side board plaite, noe plaites or dishes and but few salvers.' Presumably Lord Chesterfield was misinformed as to the effect of the 1697 law and disposed of his plate before discovering its true nature.

In order that silver plate made to the new standard should be readily distinguished from sterling standard silver, new hall-marks were introduced at the same time; in the wording of the act: 'the worker's mark to be expressed by the first two letters of his sur-

[1] *The Journeys of Celia Fiennes*, ed. C. Morris, London 1947, p. 171.

name, the marks of the mystery or craft of the Goldsmiths, which, instead of the Leopard's Head and the Lion, shall for this plate be the figure of a woman, commonly called Britannia and the figure of a lion's head erased, and a distinct variable mark to be used by the warden of the said mystery, to denote the year in which such plate is made.' Thus was introduced what is commonly called the Britannia standard, which was to persist until 1720, covering all but the first ten years of the period of this book. The greater purity of the silver used at this period meant that it was somewhat softer, and the terms of the Wrought Plate Act of 1719, which reintroduced the sterling standard, implied that vessels made from silver plate of the old standard had been more serviceable and durable than those made from Britannia standard silver. The appearance of such vessels at the present time does not, however, seem to lend any support to this suggestion; no difference is apparent in the condition of plate made of sterling or Britannia standard silver.

According to the terms of the Act of 1697 all working goldsmiths had to register and use marks consisting of the first two letters of their surnames. The list of marks registered at this time, together with the names of the goldsmiths to whom they belonged, has been preserved at Goldsmiths' Hall, as have been the records of all marks taken out subsequently. Not all the marks registered in 1697 were in fact new marks, as some goldsmiths had already been using marks consisting of the first two letters of their surnames. A few other pre-1697 marks have been attributed to goldsmiths with varying degrees of certainty, but it is only from 1697 onwards that we can definitely attribute pieces of wrought plate to their makers. The mark on a piece of this period is that of the plate-worker in whose workshop it was made. As is still the case in the goldsmiths' trade, many craftsmen did not have their own shop but sold their plate to a retailer who was then often a banker as well. Of the designers of late seventeenth and early eighteenth-century plate we know nothing apart from what is to be found in the foreign pattern books of the period. Whether these had much currency in England is not known, but there is little evidence of their being copied by English plate-workers. Of the engravers we do, however, know a certain amount as a few engravers' account books as well as the pattern books they published have come down to us. One French pattern book was re-issued in London in 1676 under the title 'A New Booke of Fries Work Inv$^t$ by J. le Pautre' and it was from this publication that the chased and engraved decoration on the dish (Pl. 61) was derived.

Apart from their adherence to designs which had been current in their own country, the Huguenots also preserved their identity by using in England marks of a type similar to those they had employed in France. The Parisian goldsmiths employed a mark consisting of their initials combined with a fleur-de-lys and possibly some other device surmounted by a crown. Amongst those who entered marks incorporating a crown in this period were Pierre Platel, Peter Archambo, Pierre Harache, Louis Laroche, John Le Sage and Philip Rainaud. The fleur-de-lys either above or below the initials was used by Augustine Courtauld, Edward Feline, Pezé Pilleau, Abraham Roussel and David Willaume. Louis Cuny, Jacob Margas and Mark Paillet combined crowned initials of the French type with a fleur-de-lys.

By a peculiar oversight the Act of 1697 did not provide any new series of marks for the provincial assay offices, and the provincial makers were faced with the necessity of sending their plate up to the London Goldsmiths' Hall for marking. The Britannia Standard (Provincial Offices) Act of 1700 empowered certain provincial assay offices to use the Britannia standard marks together with the arms of the city where assay took place, but in fact Britannia standard provincial plate is of extreme rarity. The only provincial assay offices that were marking any quantity of plate during our period were Exeter, Chester and York.

The Britannia standard was not abolished by the Wrought Plate Act of 1719, as this measure left it open to the goldsmith to use plate of either Britannia or sterling standard and some goldsmiths, such as Paul de Lamerie, did in fact continue to use the higher standard, in spite of the higher cost. The purpose of limiting the quantity of new plate made was now to be achieved by a tax of 6d. per ounce on all new plate. In a broadsheet which was published at the time against the introduction of the tax, we obtain an interesting piece of evidence as to the rate charged by the plate-worker for making silver vessels. 'And if 6d per oz. be laid on Plate, the manufacturer must, for all weighty Plate, pay as much, or more, than he receives for the Fashion.'[1] The tax was in fact

---

[1] Judging by the figures quoted below (p. 78) 6d. an ounce would be a very low figure indeed for fashion; it may well be that the author of the broadsheet did not hesitate to strengthen his case by exaggeration.

enforced, but such was the prosperity enjoyed by the mercantile and landed classes in the eighteenth century that it had no more effect in decreasing the amount of plate commissioned than had the earlier device of the Britannia standard. It was and continued to be the practice for the wealthy to lay up a large part of their wealth in plate.

The Wrought Plate Act of 1719 also required the goldsmiths to adopt new marks in place of those which had been introduced in 1697. Instead of the first two letters of the surname, the new marks consisted of the initials of the first name and of the surname. Some goldsmiths reverted, therefore, to the marks used in their workshops before 1697. Plate made after 1719 to the Britannia standard was still marked with the stamp consisting of the first two letters of the surname, so those goldsmiths who continued to produce higher standard plate had two different makers' marks in use.

The imposition of the plate tax of 6d. per ounce led to a dishonest practice on the part of some goldsmiths that has caused many problems to collectors of more recent times. On large pieces of plate the amount of tax payable was quite considerable; it was collected when the piece of plate was submitted for assay. There were two ways in which the tax might be circumvented, apart from the obvious one of omitting to have the piece marked at all. One was to remove the mark from a piece of plate which was to be melted and to re-use it on a new piece. Such pieces can often be recognized by the fact that they bear a date letter some years earlier than the style in which they are made. The second method was to send a small piece of plate to the Hall to be assayed and marked and then to use it in the construction of a much larger one. In order to carry out this device successfully it was necessary that the large piece should have a bottom of relatively small dimensions, so that the piece of silver bearing the mark should cover it completely. If the small piece with the mark were to be set into a larger piece it would have been necessary to solder it in position and the difference in colour of the solder and the surrounding metal would have revealed the fraud. The pieces which are most likely to have transposed marks are, therefore, such objects as two-handled cups, tea-kettles, teapots and coffee-pots. On such pieces the join of the added plate bearing the mark could be concealed by the junction between the moulded foot and the body.

## Goldsmiths and the Hall-mark

A number of pieces referred to in this work are described as being unmarked or as bearing the maker's mark only. In some cases these pieces remained unmarked because the maker had flouted the regulations of the Goldsmiths' Company, perhaps in order to avoid paying the tax, perhaps because as an alien he was not allowed to have his pieces assayed and marked. Another circumstance should, however, be mentioned which certainly gave rise to the production of much unmarked plate. As fashions in plate changed it was the custom to hand over quantities of worn or old-fashioned plate for re-fashioning according to more modern styles. When a client handed over a quantity of old plate for re-fashioning, it may well have seemed unnecessary to submit the new pieces for assay since they were made from plate which had been assayed and had borne the hallmark. Such pieces were in any case returned directly to the client and did not come into the course of trade at all. There was, therefore, no risk for the goldsmith of being found out and fined by the Goldsmiths' Company for selling unassayed plate.

# CHAPTER IV

# List of Plate and Vessels
# Commonly in Use

The forty years covered by this book can most conveniently be divided into two periods, firstly 1688 to 1702, covering the reign of William and Mary jointly and subsequently of William III alone, and secondly, 1702 to 1727, the reigns of Queen Anne and George I. During the first period we find the Carolean style with its elaborate embossed ornament in a rather provincial Baroque taste gradually giving way to the purer French forms introduced by the Huguenots. During the second period after 1702, Carolean ornament has completely disappeared, though the William and Mary ornament, based on arrangements of parallel or spiral fluting, survived amongst the English-born goldsmiths. While the Huguenot taste predominated, many English goldsmiths adopted a version of it which was stripped of all ornament, based on octagonal or hexagonal plan and decorated with stepped mouldings only. Towards the end of the period the two styles had merged and we find engraved and cast ornament applied equally by both Huguenot and English-born goldsmiths. Five possible versions of each particular vessel can, therefore, be found during this period, as follows:

1. Carolean survival with floral embossing and, more rarely, flat-chased chinoiseries; invariably the work of English-born goldsmiths.

2. William and Mary with embossed fluting and gadrooning, running either vertically or spirally; with few exceptions the work of English-born goldsmiths.

3. Huguenot with much cast applied ornament and a strongly manifested plastic sense; with the exception of a few English-born goldsmiths who followed the Huguenot style, the work of Huguenots.

[30]

4. Queen Anne, octagonal, hexagonal or circular forms without ornament, other than stepped mouldings and faceted surfaces; the work of either English-born or Huguenot goldsmiths, the former preponderating.

5. Early Georgian with profuse applied or engraved ornament on octagonal or hexagonal forms; equally the work of English-born or Huguenot goldsmiths.

## PLATE USED IN THE SERVICE OF WINE AND BEER

### 1. *Standing cups*

To judge by the number of surviving examples, one of the most popular pieces of plate in this period was the two-handled cup and cover, which succeeded the handle-less standing covered cup as the standard piece of presentation plate. The latter still survived, but hardly in domestic use. In the City Companies, where tradition died hard, we find them being presented even in the early eighteenth century, as, for example, the beautiful cup of 1705 by Benjamin Pyne belonging to the Worshipful Company of Pewterers (Pl. 1). Though the standing cup was on its way out as a piece of plate, the form of this particular cup is of great distinction and the applied straps around the lower part of the body give an appearance of strength and stability far better suited to the form than the restless Baroque ornament of some of the earlier standing cups. Smaller wine cups for individual use were by this period obsolete, having been displaced by the less expensive glass drinking vessels.

### 2. *Two-handled cups*

The form of the two-handled cup had already been evolved before the beginning of our period. The earliest examples date back, indeed, to the middle years of the seventeenth century. By 1688, the earlier pear-shaped body had been replaced by one with almost parallel sides, but during our period there was further progress in its design. The two-handled cup by John Boddington of 1697, belonging to Trinity College, Cambridge (Pl. 2), shows the English form with typical William and Mary ornament. The Huguenot form of the same date has a slightly narrower body and, a more conspicuous distinction, handles of harp-shape (Pls. 3, 4, 6), instead of those based on an S-curve of the Boddington cup. In

[31]

spite of the initial popularity of the harp-shaped handle amongst the Huguenot makers, it was eventually discarded in favour of the more traditional S form (Pl. 7). The austere but admirably proportioned applied palm leaf or strap ornament gave a sense of dignity to the Huguenot cups that was lacking in the English ones with their more mouvementé spiral fluting or gadrooning. A Huguenot cup such as that in Pl. 3 or Pl. 6 combines most effectively the formal character, appropriate for a piece of presentation plate, with grace and nobility of form. An interesting essay by a Huguenot maker in the English manner is shown in Pl. 4, a covered cup of 1702 by Louis Cuny. The vertical fluting is executed in the best Anglo-Dutch manner, though the bold harp-shaped handles point to a Huguenot origin. The cup and cover of 1692[1] belonging to Normanton Church, Yorkshire, is an equally good example of a Huguenot-style cup made by an English-born goldsmith. It is attributed to Benjamin Bathurst; both cover and body are decorated with cut-card foliage enriched with beaded ribs. The gadrooned borders and domed cover look very Huguenot in design.

The Carolean covered cup usually had a flat or nearly flat cover, but the cover gradually increased in height until by the 1720's a pronounced dome had developed (Pl. 8). At the same time, to match the increased height of the cover, the body was raised slightly higher off the foot by the insertion of a short stem. A suggestion of this stem can be seen in the cup of 1705 by Pierre Platel in the Ashmolean Museum (Pl. 6), and in fully developed form on the highly individual cup by Philip Rollos, 1714, one of a pair in the collection of the Marchioness of Cholmondeley (Pl. 9).

The development of the covered cup was a Huguenot achievement, but even a Huguenot sometimes nodded. Thus, the usually infallible David Willaume produced the exceptionally ugly Stanhope cup of 1713 at Trinity Hall, Cambridge.[2] The Huguenot cup was usually decorated with applied vertical straps or leaves, and it is of interest to follow the evolution of these ornaments, of which the Huguenot makers produced a never-failing variety. Applied decoration around the lower part of the bowl had already appeared in the form of cut-card work well before the beginning of our period, and before the end of the century the flat cut-card designs

[1] Ill., Cat., *Silver Treasures from English Churches*, 1955, Pl. XXIII, no. 138.
[2] Ill., E. A. Jones, *Cambridge Plate*, Pl. XLI.

were given more plastic form by the addition of ribs on top of the foliate designs. The cup of 1699 by John Chartier in the Ashmolean Museum (Pl. 3) already shows a variety of applied ornament. Thus on the cover there are applied laurel leaves with crinkly edges, while on the body palm leaves alternate with a reversed lambrequin-like ornament upon which is set a gadroon. Flat cut-card work was still found on early eighteenth-century plate but the profile of the applied sheet was more complex, being cut into intricate floral designs. The favourite forms of the early eighteenth century were the lanceolate design seen on the lower part of the John Chartier cup, the crinkly edged leaf on the cover of the same cup, and the reversed lambrequin, either flat and pierced as on the Simon Pantin cup of 1705 (Pl. 5), or strengthened by the addition of a rib or gadroon as on the Chartier cup. The next development was the use of cast straps and leaves ornamented in relief with guilloche ornament, husks or shells. The cup by Pierre Platel of 1705 in the Ashmolean Museum (Pl. 6) is decorated with leaves enriched with husks, alternating with reversed lambrequins enriched with panels of guilloche ornament. By the 1720's, when Paul de Lamerie was already producing his finest works, we find an even richer treatment of the applied ornament. Lamerie favoured a plain rib alternating with a broad strap pierced with an interlacing design and enriched with applied shells and masks (Pl. 8). His strap designs were usually in two layers, the upper being pierced to show the lower one below. His strapwork with shells and medallion heads owed much to French goldsmiths' design books of the early eighteenth century. The area between the ribs was given a finely matted surface, the upper border of which was shaped, corresponding to the outline of the straps. Most goldsmiths adhered to the standard form an early version of which is David Willaume's cup of 1705 (Pl. 7). A variant form is to be seen in the monumental pair of covered cups of 1714 by Philip Rollos belonging to the Marchioness of Cholmondeley. The maker has evidently drawn upon all the resources of his workshop to produce these cups, one of which is illustrated in Pl. 9.

A number of other vessels were decorated with strapwork, the evolution of which followed the same course in each case. Amongst the vessels thus treated were ewers, wine-coolers, wine-jugs and flagons and punch-bowls. The most notable improvement in design of the late seventeenth-century covered cup as opposed to the Carolean type was the new form of handle. Whereas the handles of the latter had been light and thin, those of the cups of our period were of massive proportions, their bulk matching the size of the cup. They were not always cast solid, as had been those of Carolean cups, but were sometimes hollow, worked up from flat plate. From about 1700, the two-handled cup almost invariably had a substantial girdle running round the body above the tops of the applied straps. On the earlier cups this girdle might be gad-rooned, but this enrichment was soon abandoned in favour of a plain moulding.

### 3. *Monteiths and punch-bowls*

The Monteith, which had been introduced during the reign of Charles II, was replaced early in the eighteenth century by the punch-bowl. The Monteith was a specifically English type of vessel and the traditional English methods of ornament, consisting of Baroque scrollwork embossed in relief and cast cherubs' heads applied round the rim, persisted into the eighteenth century (Pl. 18). The difference in quality between the masks on Huguenot work and the coarsely modelled cherubs' heads on the rims of Monteiths is particularly striking. The body of the Monteith was sometimes plain and sometimes enriched with vertical fluting in the Dutch manner (Pl. 19A), but in either case it appears curiously unsophisticated in comparison with contemporary Huguenot work. It was indeed the most Carolean-looking of all early eighteenth-century plate. An intermediate stage intervened between the Monteith and the punch-bowl, namely that the rim around the top with the indentations for glasses was formed separately and could be removed, thus converting the vessel into a punch-bowl. The Huguenot goldsmiths produced a form of punch-bowl with applied vertical straps while the English taste was expressed in an absolutely plain form, devoid of all ornament other than the engraved armorials. Whereas the Monteith usually had a large and handsome pair of swing handles, the punch-bowl proper often lacked these, relying entirely upon proportion and the sheen of the metal for its effect. The most imposing of all punch-bowls is one presented by Sir Watkin Williams Wynn to Jesus College, Oxford in 1732. Made by John White in 1726, it is one of the largest of its kind, having a capacity of 4 gallons (Pl. 19B). It thus exceeds in size, though not in beauty, that belonging to the Corporation of Stamford,[1] which was made in 1685 and has a capacity of $3\frac{1}{2}$ gallons.

### 4. *Wine cisterns*

The largest vessels used in the service of wine were the wine-coolers or cisterns and their companion fountains. They were usually made en suite, the former intended to rest on the floor while the latter stood on a side-table. They were, however, also used for washing plates and dishes, as more than one contemporary reference shows. Thus, in one of the early wills[2] made by Sarah, first Duchess of Marlborough, she bequeathed to her grand-daughter, Lady Diana Spencer, later Duchess of Bedford, 'the little cistern for the sideboard and the fountain to hold the water that goes into it'. The 1721 inventory of the royal plate, of which two copies are preserved in the Public Record Office,[3] also suggests the more humble function of washing up as the purpose of these magnificent pieces of plate. The Treasury copy of this inventory refers to one fountain and one small cistern in the Jewel Office Store, but the Lord Chamberlain's copy, referring to the same objects, describes them as a 'fountain and washer'. The cistern or cooler was normally used to contain bottles of wine packed in ice, thus functioning as a giant ice pail.

Few wine-coolers and even fewer wine fountains have survived. The great weight of plate they contained has condemned most of them to the melting pot, but it is probable that they were not so uncommon in the late seventeenth and early eighteenth centuries. Now they are only to be found in the possession of a few noble houses and in public institutions, but the coats of arms engraved on some surviving examples show them to have been made for lesser noblemen. The enormous wine-cooler and fountain of 1708 by David Willaume (Pls. 23, 27), now the property of the Duke of Brunswick, were originally made for an Irish peer, the Earl of Meath, a cooler now in the Hermitage bears the arms of the Earl of Scarsdale (Pl. 24), while the Earl of Bristol not only owned one himself but gave another to his son, Lord Hervey, in 1716.

---

[1] Ill., Cat., *Corporation Plate*, 1952, Pl. XXIX, no. 83.
[2] I am obliged to the Rt. Hon. The Earl Spencer for this reference from un-published papers in his possession.
[3] Ref. nos. TI/CXXXV and LC5/114.

## List of Plate and Vessels Commonly in Use

The Carolean form of wine-cooler was fairly standardized and survived into our period; it is well represented by that made in 1694 by the court goldsmith, George Garthorne, which now belongs to the Bank of England. It is of oval shape and the body bulges out to form a series of lobes or gadroons separated by panels of husks. Above the bulging body is a broad vertical band of foliage intended to be seen from within, and over this projects the flat rim with gadrooned edge. At each end is a large loop handle hanging from a lion's mask, and the whole is supported on four massive claw and ball feet (Pl. 20).

This design was old-fashioned for 1694 and by 1697 we have already the most elegant wine-cooler of that year made by Pierre Harache and later presented by Queen Anne to the Barber-Surgeon's Company (Pl. 21). Here the form has become more reposeful and dignified; the handles continue the sweep of the body and the ornament is adequate but restrained. It is interesting to note that Pierre Harache used the same handle design for this wine-cooler as he employed on a ewer now belonging to the Vintners' Company (Pl. 34A). In his exhaustive study of wine-coolers, Dr. N. M. Penzer[1] lists 22 surviving from the first quarter of the eighteenth century; the fact that so many should survive points to their having been more common among the nobility that might be expected. Of these 15 were made by Huguenot goldsmiths; Philip Rollos heads the list with five, followed by David Willaume with four. Those examples that were not made by Huguenots were the work of those English-born goldsmiths, such as Anthony Nelme or Benjamin Pyne, who worked in the Huguenot manner. It is probable that each wine-cooler was originally accompanied by a wine fountain, but the latter, being less useful than the cooler, which could also be used for rinsing dishes or glasses, has more frequently been melted.

The wine-cooler was often of immense dimensions; that in the Hermitage Museum, Leningrad (Pl. 22), bearing the arms of Evelyn Pierrepoint, first Duke of Kingston, by Philip Rollos, weighs over 3,500 ounces, another belonging to the Marquess of Exeter by the same maker, dating from about 1710 (maker's mark only) weighs nearly 3,700 ounces. Though there is much variety of detail, the early eighteenth-century wine-coolers conform to a

[1] *Apollo*, Vol. LXVI, September 1957, ps. 39–46, 'The Great Wine Coolers' —II.

single type. They are oval and stand on an oval base, or less frequently on four feet, as that belonging to the Marquess of Exeter by Philip Rollos.[1] The lower part of the vessel is often embossed with heavy gadroons, as was the William and Mary type (Pl. 20), and the lip is treated en suite. There are large swing handles, hanging either from lions' masks or from figures based on the supporters of the owner's coat of arms, as in the fine wine-cooler in Pl. 23.

No wine-coolers of this period survive amongst the royal plate, and only one is mentioned in the 1721 inventory. William III had four made after the arrival of Queen Mary from the Hague in 1689[2] but not one of these lasted even the thirty odd years until 1721, unless they were sent to Hanover by George I. They were all over 1,000 ounces in weight and the cost of fashioning was 9s. per ounce, a high price, suggesting that they were richly ornamented. One of them was engraved with 346 arms at 5s. each and 186 ciphers at 1s. 2d. each. Another was purchased from the estate of the 5th Earl of Meath, but this was sent over to Hanover to form part of the Prince of Wales's plate and never returned. There are, however, two wine fountains listed in the 1721 inventory, one being the Carolean fountain kept with the Regalia in the Tower of London.

## 5. *Ice pails*

The ice pail, which was a far more convenient object than the wine-cooler, was introduced before the end of the seventeenth century. It contained only a single bottle of wine but could be placed upon the table. An ice pail of 1698 belongs to the Duke of Devonshire and there is a particularly handsome pair at Ickworth, bearing the arms of the first Earl of Bristol (Pl. 25). These bear the mark of Philip Rollos but no hall-mark; the earldom was created in 1714 and they can, therefore, be dated about 1715–20. The form differs little from that still in use two centuries later. Another pair dating from 1713 by Louis Mettayer in the Ashmolean Museum are engraved with the royal arms and originally formed part of the Speaker's plate of Sir Thomas Hanmer, Bart.

## 6. *Wine fountains*

The wine fountain is considerably rarer than the cooler. Penzer

---

[1] Ill., Penzer, op. cit., Fig. IX, p. 44.
[2] E. A. Jones, *Old English Plate of the Emperor of Russia*, p. xliv.

records only four dating from the first quarter of the eighteenth century; of these three are by Huguenot goldsmiths. In form they recall immensely over-grown covered cups, with swing handles instead of the S- or harp-shaped ones of the cup. Their great size made them a suitable vehicle for elaborate ornament in the form of numerous mouldings, bands of gadrooning and fluting and applied brackets (Pl. 26). On the more important examples the heraldic bearings of the owner were not engraved but applied in high relief, an inconvenient circumstance when the vessel changed hands. Such applied details could not be removed without extensive remodelling of the piece, which accounts for the peculiar combination of the Prince of Wales's Feathers and an earl's coronet on the fountain in Pl. 27. This piece was purchased along with its companion cooler for the use of George II, when Prince of Wales, after the death in 1715 of its first owner, Chamber, 5th Earl of Meath.

### 7. *Wine bottles*

The pilgrim flask, which had retained much the same shape and size since the Middle Ages, appeared in vastly enlarged guise in the late seventeenth century. Such flasks or bottles were hardly intended for use but, like the outsize sideboard dishes of the period, for display. They received more or less elaborate ornament and were mostly, though not exclusively, made by the Huguenots. The largest of all,[1] weighing 483 ounces, is part of the royal plate. It is unmarked, but dates from the late seventeenth century and was probably made by Anthony Nelme, the maker of a very similar pair belonging to the Duke of Devonshire at Chatsworth. It now serves as a wine fountain, a tap, together with a certain amount of applied ornament, having been added by Paul Storr for the Prince Regent in the early nineteenth century. The pair of bottles presented to the Duke of Marlborough along with other plate by Queen Anne after the battle of Blenheim are not much smaller. They bear the London hall-mark for 1701 and maker's mark of John Goode and weigh together 645 ounces. The most beautiful of these wine bottles are perhaps the pair belonging to Eton College; these are by Pierre Harache and bear the London hall-mark for 1699 (Pl. 29). The coat of arms is a later addition. The fashion for these huge pieces of plate hardly outlasted the reign of Queen

[1] Ill., E. A. Jones, *Windsor Castle Plate*, Pl. XXXII.

Anne, the latest recorded being the pair at Chatsworth, which date from 1715. In spite of the higher cost of plate at the time these weigh no less than 799 ounces.

## 8. *Tankards*

Tankards followed much the same course of development as cups. Apart from the fashion for flat-chased chinoiseries during the 1680's and the Scandinavian fashion followed for a while in York, both of which fall for discussion in an earlier volume in this series, the Carolean tankard had been devoid of ornament other than the heraldic bearings of the owner within crossed palm leaves. The cast handles of the average Carolean cup were rarely used on the tankards, which nearly always had good substantial ones of wrought plate. During the first part of our period, the English-born makers produced either a completely plain tankard with slightly tapering body, flat lid, S-scroll handle and volute thumb-piece (Pl. 12A), which differed hardly at all from the Carolean type, or one with spiral fluting and gadrooning around the lower part of the body, bold cabled girdle and Baroque cartouche with scale-work (Pl. 13B), the counterpart of that already described with reference to the two-handled cup. Lavish use was made of cut-card work on the more important presentation tankards, as on the example of 1701 by Joseph Ward at Jesus College, Oxford (Pl. 13A), but this type of ornament, as also the beaded rat-tail running down the back of the handle, did not long survive the turn of the century. The form that succeeded this was austere in the extreme, though the cylindrical body was broken by a moulded girdle just above the point of junction of the lower end of the handle (Pl. 15A).

The tankard was not a vessel with which the Huguenots would have been at all conversant, since beer-drinking was not usual in most parts of France. Few of the tankards of this period bear the marks of the Huguenot goldsmiths, but those few that do usually differ in one way or another from the standard English type. The Huguenots modified the latter by rounding the lower part of the body instead of running up straight from the base moulding, or by setting a baluster finial in the centre of the lid. The exceptionally handsome tankard by Samuel Margas of 1713 belonging to the Ironmongers' Company illustrates both these points (Pl. 14B). The lion thumb-piece and the lion feet were not an exclusively

Huguenot feature; the former can be seen on the Jesus College tankard referred to above, and they were introduced before the beginning of our period. During the first decade of the eighteenth century, the cover of the tankard was heightened as was that of the two-handled cup, eventually developing a definite dome, as in the tankard of 1713 by Matthew Lofthouse (Pl. 15A). So general did this fashion for the dome-topped tankard become that a number of late seventeenth-century tankards, made before the dome appeared, suffered the fate of having their flat covers domed out to this far from beautiful shape. It was evidently felt that the flat lid did not balance the massive body of the tankard, but the Huguenot device of raising the centre slightly and setting a baluster finial on it to give added importance was a much happier solution of the problem (Pl. 12B).

### 9. *Mugs*

The mug of this period was a reduced version of the tankard, normally without a cover, and held half a pint (Pl. 15B). The two main varieties corresponded to the two types of tankard turned out by the English goldsmiths but a great many different forms were made, some of rather poor workmanship. The Huguenots also devised an individual form of mug, supplied with a cover and baluster finial. An example of 1703 by John Chartier is illustrated in Pl. 17A, but such pieces were not made in any quantity. A particularly elegant form with everted lip and moulded girdle is known in a few examples only.[1]

### 10. *Flagons and jugs*

Large flagons of the type that formed part of the altar plate of the time were still sometimes made for secular use, though few have survived, and most of these as a result of subsequent presentation to a church. Their form was sometimes most conservative, as in the case of the pair of 1718 by Edward Holaday, which were presented to the Mercers' Company by the Corporation of the Mines Royal (Pl. 11). The large skirted base on these flagons is characteristic of pieces dating from the third quarter of the seventeenth century. Jugs of various sizes were also used in the service of beer. They usually had pear-shaped bodies and might be either

[1] A mug of this type of 1699 by George Garthorne is illustrated by G. B. Hughes, *Small Antique Silverware*, Fig. 180.

covered,[1] as in the case of the fine jug by Simon Pantin of 1711 belonging to Jesus College, Oxford (Pl. 33), or without cover (Pl. 30B). The latter type was either provided with a separate spout applied to the body, or the spout was wrought from the lip. The handle was of S form, though on some of the Huguenot examples we find the more complex double scroll.

### 11. *Salvers*

Salvers or tables, as they were called in the early eighteenth century, were dishes, sometimes of considerable size and weight, standing on a central foot. In form they were merely larger versions of the church paten and were often the vehicle for much ingenuity on the part of the engraver. The circumstances in which they were used are not altogether certain. During the Carolean period one finds covered cups or even tankards with a salver en suite, and the purpose of the latter was presumably to carry the cup or tankard when it was offered to another person. The salvers of our period were not, however, normally accompanied by a cup[2] and it is probable that they had become simply large and decorative pieces of sideboard plate, as for instance, the very large salver made by John Le Sage for Philip Stanhope, 4th Earl of Chesterfield, now in the Victoria and Albert Museum (Pl. 39). It is significant that the pieces of plate made out of the defaced seal of an officer of state took the form of a salver. This would suggest that its purpose was not predominantly functional. These salvers made from seals are discussed in the chapter dealing with engraved plate (p. 71).

### PLATE USED FOR THE TOILET

The toilet service of the early eighteenth century constituted one of the most impressive assemblages of plate of the time. During the Carolean period its extent had been developed but it could still be laid out on the dressing table; by the early eighteenth century,

[1] It is possible that these covered jugs were used for some other beverage than beer. A number have survived in college common-rooms and there seems no doubt, therefore, that they were used for some form of alcoholic beverage. The fact that the handle was entirely of silver shows that the liquid they were intended to contain was cold.

[2] The list of plate stored in the Jewel Office for 20th March 1705, includes, however, 'one coffee pott and table', showing that other vessels than those used in the service of wine might be accompanied by a salver.

however, it could hardly have been accommodated on a single table (Pl. 38). The most complete surviving service is that ordered by the Rt. Hon. George Treby from Paul de Lamerie as a wedding gift for his wife, Charity Hele, now in the Ashmolean Museum, Oxford.[1] It consists of twenty-eight pieces, comprising a silver-mounted table mirror, a ewer, a pair of pomade pots, two large and two small circular boxes, two large and one small rectangular casket, two whisks and two clothes brushes, four square trays, a pair of candlesticks, two canisters, a pair of snuffers and tray and two glass jars with silver covers. Though all supplied by one goldsmith and hall-marked in the same year, 1724, the ornament of all the pieces is not consistent and one has the impression that the set has been put together from what was available in the gold-smith's stock. Such services were supplied in a fitted leather case but this has rarely survived; indeed the toilet services themselves have usually been broken up and dispersed. Though the whole of the Treby service is by one maker, this was not always the case. Some London retail goldsmiths made up services from pieces obtained from other working goldsmiths, and it is not, therefore, unusual to find more than one goldsmith represented in such a service.

While the Treby service is generally regarded as one of the finest in existence, it is equalled by another service made by David Willaume and Augustine Courtauld in the following year, 1725, and now belonging to Viscount Cowdray. This service was formerly in Russia and bears the cipher of Princess Maria Feodorovna of Württemberg.[2] Not only is this Willaume service very similar in composition to the Treby service, but the design of the cast panels on the pomade pots is identical. Presumably Willaume borrowed the moulds from de Lamerie, but it may be that both goldsmiths had recourse to a third one for this purpose. The occurrence of identical designs on pieces bearing the marks of different goldsmiths underlines the difficulty of distinguishing between the styles of different masters working at the same time.

The original bill for the Treby service is preserved and is worth quoting here[3] as it gives interesting contemporary evidence as to the purpose of some of the pieces.

[1] Ill., E. A. Jones, *Farrer Collection*, Pls. XXXVII–XLI and P. A. S. Phillips, *Paul de Lamerie*, Pls. XXXI–XXXIV.
[2] Toronto Exhibition, cat. no. F41.
[3] Reproduced in facsimile, Phillips, op. cit., Fig. 18.

| | £ | s. | d. |
|---|---|---|---|
| Delivred a fyne Sett of Dressing plate, fynely Carved all over & Chased, weighing together 637 oz. 18 dwt., at 6s. 2d. per oz. . . . | 196 | 13 | 10 |
| Fashion 5s. per oz. . . . . . | 159 | 10 | 0 |
| Engraving of all ye Armes, &c. . . . | 6 | 6 | 0 |
| For ye Glase and wooden frame . . . | 5 | 5 | 0 |
| For ye two Glasses for whater . . . | 0 | 16 | 0 |
| For Lyning of ye two Comme Boxes, ye 2 Draughts, and that of ye Juelle Tronk . . | 2 | 2 | 0 |
| For ye Locke to ye Juelle Tronke . . . | 1 | 1 | 0 |
| For ye Tronk for all ye Dresing Plate . . | 5 | 5 | 0 |
| For 4 Brushes to Clean ye Cloth and Commes . | 0 | 15 | 0 |

Since the toilet service was part of the personal equipment of the owner it received particularly rich treatment, hence the high charge of 5s. per ounce for fashion.

## 1. *Ewers*

Although the general use of forks had relegated the large ewer and basin to the sideboard as purely ornamental plate, their production continued until the mid-eighteenth century. While little practical use could be found for the largest sizes, the small ewers were used for ablutions and the complete toilet service usually included both basin and ewer (Pl. 38). The five silver basins and ewers which, according to the 1721 inventory of the royal plate, were kept in the St. James's Lodgings, were doubtless used for this purpose. Two main types of ewer were made during this period, both of them of French origin. The Carolean ewer had a body of beaker form on a high truncated stem and, apart from its scrolled handle, was not decorated. The first of the imported types was rounded instead of being cut off square; it stood on a low baluster foot and had a harp-shaped handle. This type was plain, or enriched at the most with gadrooned ornament, as in the example of 1694 by Thomas Issod at Knole, engraved with the arms of George III (Pl. 30A). This particular ewer is unusual in that it has also a cover with a small knob handle in the centre, as has a very similar example by Francis Garthorne which still remains amongst the royal plate.[1]

The true helmet-shaped ewer was introduced before the end of

[1] Ill., E. A. Jones, *Windsor Castle Plate*, Pl. XXI.

the century; the very fine one of 1697 by Pierre Harache already shows the type in its fully evolved form (Pl. 34A). The body is formed like a deep circular inverted helmet; it stands on a baluster foot and has an open scroll handle or, more rarely, a harp-shaped one.[1] Once introduced, this type remained standard as long as ewers were made, and some of the most magnificent pieces of show plate of the eighteenth century took this form, amongst them the solid gold ewer and basin of 1701 made by Pierre Platel for the Duke of Devonshire and still preserved at Chatsworth.[2] Ewers gave great scope for plastic ornament, and usually received imaginative treatment, particularly those intended for display rather than use. A mask of classical form or a shell was usually set under the lip (Pls. 34A, B), while the handle was formed as a human figure or an animal. The grotesque element, which had been present in some Carolean plate, is completely absent. The same combinations of cut-card ornament and applied straps, which have already been described above in relation to covered cups, were used in the decoration of ewers; the rich example by David Willaume in the Victoria and Albert Museum shows cut-card ornament of a particularly sophisticated type combined with reversed lambrequins (Pl. 34B). The plainer ones, such as that made by Edward Vincent in 1713 belonging to Trinity College, Oxford, rely for their effect on graceful form, the elegant shape of the body being answered by a double scroll handle with lion's head terminal (Pl. 35B).

## 2. *Basins*

Two types are found, corresponding to the large and small sizes of ewer. The large ewer was by this period a piece of ceremonial rather than useful plate, and the large basin that went with it seems to have been designed as a piece of decorative sideboard plate also. At the beginning of this period these large basins were of plain design and the omission of the central boss, which had been a feature of the earlier type, emphasized the plainness. Before the end of the century the basin began to receive more decorative treatment in the form of a heavily gadrooned border. Subsequently this border became richer by the addition of applied strapwork and other relief ornament. The main decorative feature

---

[1] Compare ewer of 1702 with harp handle, E. A. Jones, *Cambridge Plate*, Pl. LXII.

[2] See Frontispiece.

was, however, the elaborately mantled coat of arms of the owner, usually engraved in the centre (Pl. 64), but sometimes cast in relief and applied.

The most handsome is that made by Paul de Lamerie in 1723 for the Hon. George Treby, one of his main customers, who also commissioned from him the famous toilet service now in the Ashmolean Museum. In this case the border combines gadrooning with an inner design of shells alternating with masks against a punched ground (Pl. 62). The most imposing feature of this basin is the superbly modelled coat of arms of Treby, executed in high relief and enclosed within an elaborate Baroque cartouche surmounted by a shell and incorporating grotesque masks and classical busts within medallions (Pl. 63). These large-size basins were so shallow as to be indistinguishable from dishes, and when they are separated from their ewers it is impossible to be certain whether they were originally basins or dishes. The smaller ewers, however, were accompanied by deep basins, such as that in the great toilet service made by Benjamin Pyne for the Duke of Norfolk (Pl. 38).

### 3. Shaving jugs and basins

The jug which accompanied the shaving dish was of pear-shape and not dissimilar from the covered beer-jugs referred to above. They might, however, have the added subtlety of an oval body. That illustrated in Pl. 36B made by Anne Tanqueray has the usual Huguenot enrichments, namely gadrooned mouldings and a double scroll handle. The shaving dish was usually circular with a large bite out of of one side to accommodate the neck. Even that intended for use by the royal barber (Pl. 36A) has no ornament other than the royal arms and cipher. The shaving equipment was completed with a spherical silver box with hinged lid for the soap.

### 4. Chamber-pots

A standard piece of plate for the toilet was the chamber-pot. Though now quite rare, these once existed in large numbers. The royal inventory of 1721 surprisingly enough lists only six, but this may have been because porcelain ones imported from China had already made their appearance. In form they correspond to the modern chamber-pot.

## PLATE USED IN THE SERVICE OF TEA, CHOCOLATE OR COFFEE

### 1. *Teapots*

Teapots were first introduced only shortly before the beginning of our period, and examples dating from before the reign of Queen Anne are, therefore, extremely rare. One of the earliest forms was a close copy of the porcelain wine-pots which were at the time being imported from China for use as teapots. Only two of these are known to survive. The handsome pear-shaped type, usually and correctly known as Queen Anne, has survived in a much larger number, but none of these can be dated before 1700. It appears in two forms, that is with round (Pl. 40A) or octagonal (Pl. 40B) body and curved spout sometimes ending in a conventionalized monster's head (Pl. 41A). At first the handle was rather inconveniently set at right angles to the spout, but subsequently it took its obvious place on the opposite side of the body to the handle. The pear-shaped teapot was usually completed with a spirit lamp and stand, though this is often missing. The great majority of teapots of this period were quite plain, relying for their effect on their proportion and shape. The Huguenots tried to introduce some variety by the use of cut-card work or applied straps but the most successful are those that are unornamented. The square teapot by Anthony Nelme of 1708 is an interesting curiosity (Pl. 44A); only one other is recorded. The most monumental of the Huguenot teapots is that of 1706 by David Willaume (Pl. 42). The three rows of applied straps on the body give it an importance that is not inappropriate in view of its large size.

The pear-shaped teapot with curved polygonal spout continued in fashion until about 1720 and was made by both Huguenot and English-born goldsmiths. In their production it can fairly be said that the English goldsmiths held their own in comparison with their immigré rivals. Makers such as Samuel Wastell and William Charnelhouse seem to have specialized in them and completely mastered the possibilities of the pear-shaped form. During the second decade of the century a globular form was introduced which eventually displaced the pear-shape. It was not in fact spherical, though the Edinburgh goldsmiths produced a form which approached very close to a perfect sphere. The London form had a flattened top and the body tapered towards the ring foot. A typical globular teapot by James Smith (Pl. 44B) dates from 1719 but earlier examples are known, including a fine one of 1716 by Paul de Lamerie. The earliest known to me is that by Anthony Nelme of 1712, formerly in the collection of Sir John Noble.[1] Even the globular teapot might be given an octagonal shape as in the rare example of 1719 by the Huguenot maker, Jacob Margas (Pl. 41B).

The early eighteenth-century teapot was usually of small size and required replenishment from time to time. For this purpose a tea-kettle was provided as part of the tea equipage. These were made in a pear-shaped form corresponding to that of the teapot, and, like, the latter, were either octagonal or round. They differed in having a swing handle with turned ebony grip, hinged on each side of the cover. The spout was given a somewhat more important form by the addition of a single or double moulding at the base. They were invariably provided with a lamp and stand on three or four legs (Pl. 43), and sometimes with a separate silver tripod table as well (see p. 61).

### 2. *Coffee and chocolate-pots*

These can be dealt with together as they did not differ in form. Chocolate-pots can be distinguished by the presence of a small aperture in the lid, closed by a hinged or pivoted cover through which a stirring stick could be inserted (Pls. 50B, 52A). Two main forms were in use during this period, one with straight tapering sides (Pl. 51A), the other with a pear-shaped body (Pl. 50B); the former being preferred by the English-born goldsmiths, the latter by the Huguenots. The earliest coffee-pot had a tapering body of round section and a conical lid (Pl. 49B); this type persisted until the beginning of the eighteenth century, but was gradually superseded by a type with rounded cover which softened the rather sharp line of the earlier pattern (Pl. 52B). The plain areas of the body were often relieved with cut-card work and the top with vertical fluting (Pl. 50B). The coffee-urn in Pl. 53 shows a rare variation of this type. The pear-shape was probably a Huguenot innovation but its use was by no means confined to the Huguenot goldsmiths; see, for example, the fine chocolate-pot by Thomas Corbet of 1703 in which the familiar English features are set upon a French-type body (Pl. 50B). An octagonal body was soon introduced as an alternative to the round one; with this went an

[1] Christies, 12.xii.51, lot 94 (ill. in cat.).

octagonal cover (Pl. 51B). The tall tapering forms were not really to the taste of the Huguenots, who preferred a rounded pear-shaped body. A characteristically French version is shown in Pl. 50A, a chocolate-pot of 1705 by Pierre Platel. The flat lid and baluster handle are of unmistakably French pattern.

### 3. *Hot-water jugs*

Hot-water jugs, which went with the tea service, corresponded in form to the coffee-pot but were of smaller size, and had an applied triangular spout instead of a tubular one. Examples are illustrated in Pls. 54A, B and 55A with bodies of octagonal, square and circular section respectively.

### 4. *Milk jugs*

Milk jugs dating from this period are rare and it would seem that when tea-drinking was first introduced milk was not considered necessary; they were formed as a miniature version of the beer-jug (Pl. 48A). From the 1720's onwards they became more common. Hot-milk jugs dating from the 1720's are also known; they correspond to the cold-milk jugs but are completed with a cover and an ivory or hard-wood handle.

### 5. *Sugar bowls*

Sugar bowls dating from before 1700 are rare but not unknown; there were two main types, either round or octagonal, each being completed with a cover.[1] The cover of the round type usually had a small rim in the centre of the top, and when reversed could be used as a saucer dish (Pls. 57A, 58A). This form was copied from the Chinese tea-bowls which were being imported at the time. The cover of the octagonal type was not reversible and ended in a baluster finial (Pls. 56A, B).

### 6. *Tea-caddies*

The tea-caddy or canister, which made its appearance about the end of the seventeenth century, was during this period usually of rectangular (Pl. 46A) or hexagonal (Pl. 46B) design and received little enrichment. They were made in sets of two for green and

---

[1] A sugar bowl of 1699 by John Leach with typical English spiral gadrooning and fluting is illustrated by G. B. Hughes, *Small Antique Silverware*, Fig. 50.

bohea tea respectively,[1] sometimes with a sugar box as well, and were supplied in wooden cases covered with leather or shagreen.

## 7. *Teacups*

Silver teacups were introduced towards the end of the seventeenth century as part of the tea-drinking equipment, but were soon abandoned on account of the excessive heat-conducting qualities of silver. Very few of this period survive, but it should not necessarily be assumed that few were originally made, since they would almost inevitably have been melted when imported cups of porcelain became available. The earliest recorded pair of teacups with silver stands (if they are, in fact, teacups), are of monumental character, of very heavy metal with cut-card ornament, two S-scroll handles and profuse acanthus scroll engraved ornament (Pl. 45A). They date from 1688, and, apart from the form of the handles, which are set vertically instead of horizontally, can be described as miniature écuelles. An example of the early years of the eighteenth century is shown in Pl. 45B. A more practicable device was to use a porcelain cup with a silver saucer. Pl. 47 shows an example by David Tanqueray dating from 1718, holding in this case a beaker-cup of the type then used for coffee or chocolate. The tall cup with narrow base and wider lip might easily upset and the lower part was, therefore, enclosed within a silver frame. This construction was more usual on the Continent than in England and was a normal feature of coffee-beakers made at Meissen, Vienna and elsewhere during the eighteenth century. The engraved ornament on the inner side of the saucer is of typically French character and seems to have been copied from one of the designs in the Masson pattern book published in Paris in the early eighteenth century. Page 5 of this publication[2] includes a number of designs for *Soucoupes rondes a Caffé* as well as a *Gobelet à Caffé*. No silver coffee-cups of English origin are recorded.

## 8. *Tea trays*

The tea service was set on a silver tray, or, as it was then known, table. These might be hexagonal or hexafoil, octagonal, or octofoil or of even more complex design (Pls. 59A, B). The marking-out of

[1] The Jewel Office Deliveries for 1709 refer to 'one Bohea tea pott' suggesting that a special type of teapot may have been used.
[2] Reproduced, *Œuvres de Bijouterie et Joaillerie des XVIIᵉ et XVIIIᵉ Siècles*, Pl. 30.

the lobed profile and application of the curved or angular borders was a process calling for great skill on the part of the craftsman. The most attractive feature of the tray was, however, the engraved coat of arms with elaborate mantling or cartouche which occupied the centre.

### 9. *The dinner service*

The dinner service consisted only of plates and dishes of matching design. The large services with tureens and other vessels all decorated en suite were an invention of the latter part of the eighteenth century. Tureens, sauce-boats and casters were already in use, but they do not seem to have been made in sets with the plates and dishes.

Dinner plates and dishes were for the most part quite simple, being circular, either with or without a plain moulding running around the edge. Some more important services had gadrooned edges, described as 'knurled' in the contemporary inventories, as for instance, a set of dishes engraved with the arms of William III, formerly belonging to the Duke of Devonshire[1] or the example from a private collection in Pl. 60. Octagonal plates were also made but no complete services seem to have survived. Both plates and dishes were engraved with the full arms or the crest of the owner on the rim, or, on larger dishes, in the centre.

In addition to large dishes forming part of a dinner service, very large dishes, sometimes called 'sideboard dishes', were made. These were much more elaborately treated with shaped edges and finely chased applied borders, as, for instance, that made by Paul de Lamerie in 1722, and now in the Ashmolean Museum, Oxford (Pl. 64). Such dishes were originally completed with a ewer and did not form part of large services of similarly decorated pieces; they are discussed under toilet plate above (p. 44). Fruit bowls with fluted bodies and scalloped edges, sometimes enriched with applied cast ornament, made their appearance at this time and constituted a particularly useful and attractive innovation.

A normal feature of the dinner service of the eighteenth century was the mazarine. This was a flat silver plate with decorative piercings that fitted into a larger dish and was used for straining boiled fish. The 1721 inventory of the royal plate refers to 51 of these in the scullery of St. James's Palace, but none of so early a

[1] Christies, 25.vi.58, lot 51 (ill. in cat., Pl. XV).

date is recorded. That they were used for fish is shown by the series that are still preserved amongst the royal plate; these are very attractively pierced and engraved with different kinds of fish. They date, however, from the second half of the century.

### 10. *Soup Tureens*

In form the soup tureen was a smaller version of the wine-cooler, with, of course, the necessary addition of a cover. Owing to the large amount of metal they contained, they have mostly been melted, but it is unlikely that many were made during our period. There were, according to the 1721 Inventory, only three in the scullery at St. James's. The tureen is said to have been a Huguenot innovation, but the earliest recorded example, dating from 1703, is the work of Anthony Nelme. The example illustrated (Pl. 65A), belonging to the service made for the Empress Catherine of Russia, bears the maker's mark of Simon Pantin, and like the rest of the service must have been made in or before 1726. The applied straps are characteristic of Huguenot ornament, though they are here used with little imagination. A very similar tureen[1] by Paul de Lamerie with hall-mark for 1723, belonging to the Duke of Bedford, stands on an oval stepped base instead of the volute feet of that in Pl. 65A. The Lamerie tureen has the same loop handle as that illustrated, but is in other respects a finer piece, not least because, instead of repeating the applied straps around the body, de Lamerie uses medallion heads alternating with foliate strapwork and trellis patterns.

### 11. *Sauce-boats*

Sauce-boats were an innovation of this period, though it was not till towards its end that they became at all usual. They had an attractive Baroque form, full of curves, with a spout at each end and a handle on each side. Applied moulding followed the profile of the top, and the base was of oval or octagonal form with the usual step mouldings (Pl. 65B).

### 12. *Salt cellars*

The typical salt of this period was a low vessel of rectangular, hexagonal or octagonal form, a shape admirably adapted to its function (Pls. 66B, 67A). Salts of this type were usually cast, but

---

[1] Ill., G. Taylor, *Silver*, London, 1956, Pl. 44a.

were sometimes raised from plate with soldered-in wells. Another type which survived into the early years of the eighteenth century amongst the English goldsmiths was also wrought and was known from its shape as a 'capstan' salt (Pl. 66A). One of the last of these to be made dates from 1705 and belongs to the Needlemakers' Company; the maker's mark is indecipherable. With its spirally gadrooned mouldings, the capstan salt belongs to the same family as the tankards and two-handled cups of William and Mary type discussed above.

The Huguenots introduced a more graceful form of salt, cup-shaped on a low circular base with step mouldings. The body of the salt was enriched with applied leaf or strap ornament (Pl. 67B). Another type of salt made by the Huguenots was the box salt. This type is mentioned in the royal inventory of 1721 and a few still survive amongst the royal plate. The box salt consisted of a rectangular or oval container on four scroll feet, the container being divided by a transverse partition into two compartments, presumably for pepper and salt. Each compartment was provided with a hinged lid. Nearly all the recorded examples bear the royal cipher; that illustrated in Pl. 68B, is, however, from another source.

### 13. Casters and mustard-pots

Casters were made in sets of three, a large one for sugar and a pair of smaller ones for black and cayenne pepper respectively (Pl. 79B). All three casters had pierced openings in the cover, sometimes so large that, though suitable for sugar, they allowed too much of the strong cayenne pepper to escape. Sometimes the cayenne pepper casters were used instead for mustard, and in this case the tops were either unpierced, the piercings being represented by decorative engraving, or they were fitted with an inner lining which closed the holes (Pl. 79A). Such casters with unpierced or lined covers are quite rare in comparison with the pierced types, but there can be little doubt that they must have been used as mustard-pots, for no other mustards of this period are known to exist. The earliest recorded mustard-pots, designed as such, date from 1724 and are probably the work of Jacob Margas.[1] There are, however, numerous earlier references to them. The delivery list of the Jewel Office for 30th March 1705

[1] Ill., *Antique Collector*, Vol. 28, December 1957, N. M. Penzer, 'Mustard and the first silver mustard pots'—Part II, Fig. 11, p. 231.

mentions 'one mustard pott', that for 17th December 1707 'two mustard spoons'.

Another form of caster or dredger dating from our period is found. This is straight-sided, being either cylindrical or octagonal, and is usually completed with a loop handle (Pl. 81A). This type of dredger was presumably used for spice but it may be that when the third caster of the set of three casters was used for mustard, this smaller dredger was used for cayenne pepper. These dredgers are sometimes known as muffineers but the term was not introduced until later.

During the earlier part of our period up to about 1700, casters were usually cylindrical with a gadrooned, roped or step-moulded base and a rim of matching pattern around the base of the cover. The cover was surmounted by a baluster or button finial, and was pierced with most imaginative designs based on floral, animal or other forms. Thus the remarkable set of square casters at Petworth, believed to be by John Edwards, are pierced on the dome of the cover with birds and on the frieze with chandelier ornament (Pl. 78A).

About the turn of the century other forms were introduced: vase-shaped, pyriform and baluster. In conformity with other vessels of the period, these three types were either circular or octagonal in section. It seems likely that the graceful vase form was a Huguenot innovation, while the baluster form was probably copied from the porcelain baluster vases that were being imported from China at the time to decorate the chimney-piece. The earlier casters had a flattish top enriched with a rosette of cut-card work (Pl. 79A), but the later examples dating from towards the end of our period had more pointed covers. Eventually a new form of cover construction altogether was introduced. Whereas the earlier cover had been either raised or seamed vertically, this later form consisted of a series of vertical ribs, between which were inserted panels of decorative fretwork (Pl. 78B), usually of two different patterns which were set alternately. The lower part of the cylindrical caster had been made from a single sheet of silver bent round and soldered along a vertical seam, but this method was not practicable with the vase-shaped or pyriform casters. In these, the base was made in two parts either raised or joined along a vertical seam. The joint of the upper and lower members was covered by a decoratively moulded girdle.

A problem that had to be solved by the goldsmith was that of attaching the cover to the body of the caster in such a way that it would remain in position when held upside down in use. The earliest form was the bayonet catch. In this case two lugs were soldered to the rim of the cover in such a way that they projected slightly below it. Corresponding to the lugs, two cuts were made in the rim running around the top of the body. The cover was placed on the body with the lugs over the gaps in the rim and was then given a slight turn to left or to right. A groove was cut on the inside of the lugs and in this groove the rim on the body engaged, thus holding the cover securely in position. Subsequently, it was found that a friction fit was sufficient and the lighter and smaller vase-shaped casters usually fitted in this way. A firmer grip was obtained by fitting the bottom of the cover with a sleeve of springy silver which fitted inside the top of the body.

### 14. *Cruet frames*

Cruet frames made their appearance about the end of the seventeenth century. At first they were made to hold only a pair of glass cruets, containing oil and vinegar respectively. They consisted of a flat, shaped base supported on scroll feet, surmounted by an open framework in which each bottle fitted (Pl. 80A). There was a lateral handle and each bottle was fitted with a silver cap, or, as in the case of the fine Lamerie cruet frame in the Ashmolean Museum, with silver spout and covers to which were attached double scroll handles (Pl. 80B). Besides the two-bottle frames, there were larger ones holding a set of three casters as well. The stands did not differ materially from those of the two-bottle frame, each piece of the set having its own section of base and separate ring framework. On this type the handle was no longer set at the side, but stood up vertically in the centre of the frame and ended in a loop.

### 15. *Bread baskets and épergnes*

Bread baskets were in common use but are now very rare; they are of far less decorative design than those of the mid-eighteenth century, consisting of a circular basket with pierced sides and two loop handles. An example of 1711 in the Victoria and Albert Museum is shown in Pl. 58B. Although there is a reference to an épergne in the royal inventory of 1721, no example of such early date is known to survive. It is described as follows: 'One Aparn containing one table Baskett & Cover, one foote, four salt boxes, 4 small Salts, four Branches, 6 Casters, 4 Sauceboats.' It weighed no less than 783 ounces and must, therefore, have been considerably larger than the later eighteenth-century épergnes that survive in such large numbers.

16. *Porringers*

The term porringer used to be applied to the Carolean type of two-handled cup, but it is now more correctly applied to the flat open bowls with flat pierced handles of triangular shape (Pl. 70A), which in turn were formerly known as bleeding-bowls. While they may on occasion have been used for this purpose, their normal use was the serving of porridge. While the type with single handle and no cover was distinctly English, the Huguenot goldsmiths brought with them the Continental version, which was somewhat larger, had two handles set on opposite sides to each other, and a cover (Pls. 69A, B).[1] This latter type was known as an écuelle and it was the custom on the Continent to present one filled with sweetmeats to a nursing mother. Whether they were presented on similar occasions in England is not known; they never seem to have achieved any great popularity and very few examples have survived.

*Candlesticks*

The Carolean candlestick had been manufactured from sheet silver, with hollow stem and a single seam running vertically. Candlesticks of this type with columnar stems and square or octagonal bases were still being made as late as the end of the seventeenth century (Pl. 73A, C). A rarer type of Carolean stick was based on the standard European Baroque form with baluster stem and tripod feet of volute form. These were, like their Continental counterparts, mostly used as altar candlesticks, but a set of four of small size in the Ashmolean Museum, Oxford, by Joseph Bird dating from 1700 may perhaps have been made for secular use (Pl. 73B).

From the early 1690's it became the practice to cast candlesticks instead of working them up from sheet. The stem and socket were cast in two sections and joined down the sides, the foot was also cast and applied subsequently. The form of these candlesticks,

[1] The 1702 list of plate stored in the Jewel House refers to 'Porrige potts covers'.

which were mostly of smaller size than those of the immediately preceding period, was determined by the central feature of the stem, which was usually vase-shaped, plain on the simpler pieces (Pl. 74A), but decorated with gadrooning (Pl. 74B) or even masks and shells on the richer ones. The ornament on the vase was repeated on the foot or the socket or on both. The Queen Anne or Georgian form—for the style remained popular until the reign of George II—was octagonal or hexagonal and the foot was no longer dished but rose up towards the stem (Pl. 74C). The upper face of the foot was often arranged with sixteen counter-changed facets, alternatively the facets ran evenly from socket to base. The Huguenots preferred a somewhat more decorative form; generally of circular section with a pronounced shoulder and knop cast and chiselled with gadrooning, palmettes and strapwork.

Anthony Nelme produced a number of candlesticks of individual pattern with stems formed as crudely modelled human figures. Two types are known: in one the stem takes the form of a partly draped female figure supporting a cornucopia from which projects the nozzle, in the other of a kneeling blackamoor. Examples of the first are in the Ashmolean Museum and the Bank of England,[1] of the second in the former Hearst Collection. The forms of lighting equipment of the period were so various that it is impossible to describe them all. There were, besides chamber candlesticks with circular trays, tapersticks which were miniature versions of the full-size candlesticks and, finally, wall-sconces and chandeliers, which are discussed in the chapter on silver furniture.

### Chamber candlesticks

At this period the chamber candlestick was shaped like a frying pan with a flat cast handle or a larger hollow wrought one. The somewhat battered example from Exeter College, Oxford,[2] hall-marked 1688, shows the style at the beginning of our period; that of 1703 by Louis Cuny shows the various refinements of form introduced by the Huguenots (Pl. 70B).

### Candelabra

The candelabrum, that is a central stem supporting two or more branches, is extremely rare during this period. Though a number

---

[1] Ill., Cat., *City Plate*, 1951, Pl. LV, no. 171.
[2] Ill., H. C. Moffatt, *Old Oxford Plate*, Pl. XV.

of early eighteenth-century sticks with branches survive, the branches are usually later additions made to a single candlestick of normal type. The Worshipful Company of Haberdashers own a single candlestick[1] of 1714 by Robert Timbrell and Benjamin Bently to which branches were added in 1724. The branches, which are by a different maker, have no date letter but the leopard's head erased of the Britannia standard struck four times.

### Snuffers

Pendant to the candlestick was the snuffer with its companion stand or tray. Some early examples combined a taperstick with snuffers, douter and stand, the taperstick being attached by a hook to a socket on the side of the box which held the snuffers (Pl. 75A). The base was usually octagonal, with a baluster stem supporting the box. Subsequently the taperstick was made separately. An interesting feature of the snuffers in Pl. 75B is the small S-scroll set on the top of each finger ring. These scrolls, which appear on many of the earlier English snuffers, can be traced back to the ornament in the form of a bird that was applied in this position on sixteenth-century scissors. In the course of time the bird was so far conventionalized that its original significance was probably forgotten. The manufacture of snuffers seems to have been a separate branch of the goldsmiths' trade, for if marked at all, the snuffers nearly always have a different maker's mark from that struck on the stand. Instead of being set upright in a handsome stand, the snuffer was sometimes placed flat in a shallow tray either octagonal or, more rarely, shaped to the outline of the snuffer.

### Inkstands

No reference has yet been made to a piece of plate that was frequently made of silver, namely the inkstand, then known as a standish. Two main types were in use at this period. In one the inkpot, pounce-box and wafer box were contained in a plain oblong silver box with a hinged lid and a drawer below for quill pens (Pl. 81B). This type continued in use until well into the first quarter of the eighteenth century, but the more usual Queen Anne type consisted of a rectangular tray supported on four small feet fitted with three sockets. The two outer sockets held the inkpot and

---

[1] Ill., Cat., *Livery Companies' Exhibition*, 1926, Pl. XXXIV, no. 189.

pounce-box respectively, while the central one held a bell (Pl. 82A) or a taperstick. The pens could either be laid in a trough in the tray or set vertically in apertures round the top of the inkpot. The silver bells, now often separated from the inkstand to which they originally belonged, have a remarkably pleasing ringing tone.

### Snuff and tobacco boxes

These were usually of oval shape and can be distinguished by the presence or absence of a hinge and by their size. It seems that the larger boxes which normally have pull-off lids were used for tobacco, while the smaller boxes with hinged tops were intended for snuff. The oval lid provided a space admirably suited for engraved ornament, either heraldic, or, where the owner was not armigerous, composed of a cipher made up of the owner's initials. The box was usually devoid of ornament other than engraving, but the spiral gadrooned border of the period was occasionally used on the lid. To judge by the number of silver tobacco and snuff-boxes of this period that have survived, it would seem that the gentry, who in the later eighteenth century would have used gold boxes, were at this time satisfied with silver ones (Pl. 83).

### Other plate

The various pieces of plate described in the course of this chapter do not include all those in use at this period. Amongst the articles listed in the 1702 inventory of plate stored in the Jewel Office but not treated above are the following: wine bowls (low beakers on rounded bases; assay cups (small standing cups by this time of mainly ceremonial use); dish covers; warming pans; perfume pots; ring stands; field cups and covers (probably a beaker-like cup of the type found in travelling canteens); caddinets[1] (a ceremonial stand for knife, fork and napkin).

[1] *Burlington Magazine*, Vol. C, December 1958, Charles Oman, 'Caddinets and a Forgotten Version of the Royal Arms', ps. 431-435.

# CHAPTER V

# Silver Furniture

A great deal of silver furniture had been commissioned by the nobility as well as the royal court in the Carolean period, but in our period it went out of fashion. The practice of using cast silver instead of thin silver sheet doubtless made silver furniture more expensive and the added cost due to the introduction of the Higher Standard (see p. 25) in 1697 put an end to its production for a while. The term, 'silver furniture', is not a precise one, but I am here including, besides tables and chairs, wall furniture such as looking glasses and candle-sconces, fireplace furniture such as andirons and fire-irons, and, finally, chandeliers and candlestands.

The most splendid set of silver furniture of our period is the suite of table and looking glass (Pls. 84, 85, 86), originally completed with a pair of candlestands, presented to William III by the Corporation of the City of London and now at Windsor Castle. According to the 1721 inventory of the royal plate, this suite of furniture weighed no less than 7,306 ounces, the great weight being due to the fact that, instead of being constructed of silver sheet on a wood frame, it is mostly made of solid silver. The legs and the mouldings are made of heavy cast silver, the modelling of the caryatid legs being particularly fine. An unusual feature is the pineapple which masks the crossing point of the stretchers; this is one of the earliest recorded uses in England of this particular ornamental detail. The form and decoration of both table and looking glass owe much to contemporary wooden furniture; the pendant flower and fruit swags on the latter being evidently derived from Grinling Gibbons's designs. The maker of these pieces, which rank amongst the finest silver furniture existing in any country, was Andrew Moore of Bridewell, of whom nothing is known beyond his entering his new mark at Goldsmiths' Hall in 1697. A number of other fine pieces by him survive, amongst them a pair of andirons at Windsor Castle (Pl. 85B). Apart from the silversmith's work, the William III table is outstanding also on account of the superb engraving of the royal arms and monogram which decorate the top (Pl. 84). This is discussed further on p. 69. Of another similar table made for the first Duke of Devonshire only the engraved top is preserved (see also p. 69).

Surprisingly little silver furniture is mentioned in the 1721 inventory; nothing seems to have been added since the City of London's gift to William III just mentioned. In 1721 this was at Windsor, along with two earlier suites dating from the reign of Charles II. A considerable addition was made to the royal stock of silver furniture by George II, who purchased from the Braunschweig-Wolfenbüttel line of his family two large mirrors, two tables, two pairs of torchères and five chairs all covered with silver.[1] These were all of German manufacture and dated from about 1710/20. They spent most of the eighteenth century at Windsor before finally returning to Germany in 1837, when the kingdom of Hanover was once again separated from that of England.

No silver throne has survived amongst the royal plate, nor is there any mention of one in the 1721 inventory, but there is one at the Hermitage in Leningrad which was made by a London goldsmith. This throne, together with a footstool en suite (Pl. 87), was ordered for Peter the Great, and was made by Nicholas Clausen, presumably a German immigré goldsmith, in 1713. The continental origin of its maker is apparent in its design, which is remarkably advanced for its date. The superb form of the legs with their claw and ball terminals is worthy of notice. While the legs and arms would not look out of place on a fine quality gilt gesso-covered chair of the 1720's in England, the stretchers and the deep apron are closer to contemporary German design.

A survival of somewhat later date is the silver table belonging to the Duke of Portland.[2] This is unmarked but can be dated from the elaborate heraldic cartouche of the arms of Edward Harley,

[1] Ill., and des., *Apollo*, Vol. LXVII, June 1958, J. F. Hayward, 'Silver Furniture'—IV, Fig. 1, p. 220.

[2] Ill., E. A. Jones, *Cat. of Plate at Welbeck Abbey*, Pl. XVII. There is another similar table by Augustine Courtauld in the Kremlin Museum, Moscow; this dates from 1742. Ill., E. A. Jones, *Old English Plate of the Emperor of Russia*, Pl. XXIX.

Earl of Oxford, with seventy-two quarterings, to the period shortly after 1724. It is a tea-table with rectangular top and raised edge; like the earlier tables it is made of wood covered with silver sheet, rather roughly nailed to its wooden carcase. Another tea-table, once belonging to the Dukes of Portland, is listed in their inventories but is now lost. It was gilt, weighed 131 ounces, and was sent by George I in 1722 as a christening gift to one of the first Duke of Portland's children.

The most popular piece of silver furniture of the first half of the eighteenth century was the tripod kettle stand, which was con-structed entirely of silver without a wooden frame. These stands were made in two patterns, either with a tray top or with a ring top in which the base of the kettle rested. In the former case the top could sometimes be unscrewed and used separately as a tray, while the lamp was attached to a small kettle stand.[1] In the latter, the lamp formed part of the tripod stand and only the kettle was separate. An example of this latter type of stand, but lacking the kettle, is in the Victoria and Albert Museum. It bears the crest of the Marquess of Exeter but has neither hall-mark nor maker's mark.

## Andirons

A pair of silver andirons, the plinths surmounted by figures of boys, survive amongst the royal plate (Pl. 85B). They bear the mark of Andrew Moore, the maker of the William III suite of silver furniture. They are noticeably simpler in design than the heavy Baroque types made for Charles II. In common with other forms of silver furniture, the andiron was going out of fashion during this period, mainly as a result of the increasing use of coal which was burnt in basket grates. The latest pair[2] recorded belong to the Duke of Portland at Welbeck Abbey, having formed part of the plate allowed to Robert Harley as Principal Secretary of State by a warrant of Queen Anne dated 13th November 1704. This pair at Welbeck weigh 354 ounces and were made by Philip Rollos in 1704. They take the standard form of a pedestal formed of two S-curves supporting a flaming urn. Robert Harley also received the silver garniture for a shovel and pair of tongs weighing 34 ounces, but these are not preserved.

[1] A fine example of this type, but with later tray top, was shown at the Royal Academy Winter Exhibition 1955–56, no. 212. It bears no hall-mark.
[2] Ill., E. A. Jones, *Cat. of Plate at Welbeck Abbey*, Pl. VIII.

A considerable number of andirons was still in use in the royal palaces in 1721; thus at St. James's there were a pair of large silver andirons, two pairs of smaller ones and two pairs of small dogs; at Kensington there were nine pairs of silver andirons. There was also a quantity of silver-mounted hearth furniture; namely at St. James's two pairs of silver-mounted tongs and two shovels, at Kensington five pairs of fire shovels and tongs. All these have disappeared, having presumably been melted.

Though the quantity of plate surviving from this period as a whole is very large, it cannot be assumed that the examples still in existence represent the complete range of the period or that the present distribution of silver between the various types corresponds to that obtaining when they were first made. As a rule, the smaller pieces tend to retain their usefulness while the larger ones fall out of fashion and are melted. This applies in particular to articles such as mirror frames and furniture, of which very little now survives. The royal collection of plate is particularly weak in examples of this period. One reason for the disappearance of so much plate from the royal household is to be found in the practice of allowing the Groom of the Stole and Gentleman of the Bedchamber to retain as a perquisite of office the complete furnishings of the royal bedchamber. Thus William III directed that the 'plate, utensils and goods' which belonged to his bedchamber at Kensington Palace should be for the sole use and benefit of the Groom of the Stole and Gentleman of the Bedchamber of the time being. As a result 1,860 ounces of plate passed from royal possession in 1702 to Henry Sidney, Earl of Romney, the then Groom of the Stole.

Not all the plate engraved with the royal arms that is now in the possession of English noble families necessarily belonged originally to the royal plate proper. The practice of allowing ambassadors, as well as certain other officers of state and of the court, to retain the large quantities of plate issued to them from the Jewel House continued during this period. Thus the Earl of Portland, who was appointed Ambassador Extraordinary in 1697, received a total of 6,836 ounces of plate, including 60 plates and 12 dishes, weighing 2,583 ounces, 72 trencher plates, 1,425 ounces, 3 basins and ewers, over 764 ounces, 8 salvers, 299 ounces odd, 22 mazarines in three different sizes, as well as a quantity of smaller pieces. Robert Harley, later Earl of Oxford, received no less than

8,000 ounces of official plate on his appointment as Speaker of the House of Commons in 1701 and an additional 1,000 ounces in 1704 as Principal Secretary of State.

All this official plate was engraved with the arms and cipher of the sovereign in whose reign it was granted and not with the personal arms of the recipient; it is, therefore, impossible to distinguish it from other plate received from the sovereign as a gift or legacy. An idea of the original distribution of plate can be gained from the inventory of the royal plate made in the year 1721. This inventory includes the plate in the royal palaces at St. James's, at Kensington, Hampton Court and Windsor as well as that kept in the Jewel House at the Tower of London. One of the most striking features of this inventory is the large number of sconces listed, compared with the very small number now surviving. All the silver sconces amongst the royal plate seem to date from the reign of Charles II; the cipher of William and Mary or of William III alone, which they mostly bear, being a later addition. There is, however, a set of eight of 1691 by Andrew Moore, the maker of the William III table and looking glass at Windsor described above, in the possession of the Duke of Buccleuch. Another set of eight, made by John Hodson in 1692 belongs to the Marquess of Salisbury.

In 1721 there were at St. James's Palace 28 silver sconces, 14 large looking-glass sconces weighing 3,219 ounces, 15 silver framed looking-glass sconces and 10 picture sconces, i.e. with panels embossed with figure subjects; at Kensington Palace there were 24 sconces of various kinds, at Hampton Court 18, and at Windsor Castle no fewer than 50. There were three types of wall-sconce. In the first the candle socket was attached to a shallow tray set at right angles to the reflector plate. This type is not uncommon in brass but hardly any silver examples have survived; the only one of our period recorded was made by John Barnard in 1699, and belongs to the Bank of England (Pl. 71A).

The more usual type of sconce consisted of a shaped wall-plate, to which were attached one or more sockets into which the candle branches fitted. The reflector plate might be plain or engraved with the arms or cipher of the owner or embossed with figure subjects. Sometimes it was so elaborately pierced and embossed that its efficiency as a reflector must have been seriously impaired. As the reflector plates were often constructed from quite thin plate, they were not necessarily expensive. The Huguenot sconces were, however, usually more solidly constructed of cast work and were doubtless more costly.

The English-born goldsmiths continued to produce sconces with embossed Carolean-type ornament on into the first decade of the eighteenth century. The antique boys and coarsely rendered floral detail of the sconce by John Fawdery (Pl. 71B) are typically Carolean, though dating from 1702. A number of sconces of similar type, forming part of the royal plate,[1] were made by the court goldsmith, Charles Shelley, for Charles II, the cipher of William III being a later addition. Even the Huguenots produced wall-sconces whose design recalled earlier Carolean fashion (Pl. 72B), but this was a consequence of the form of the wall or reflector plates, which positively called for embossed and pierced ornament. A less common type, which was probably of Huguenot origin, had a cast wall plate in the form of a truss or console; this type, which supported only a single branch, had a dignity of design and proportion which was not always present in the more exuberant English Baroque ones. The superb example in Pl. 72A, though characteristically Huguenot in appearance, bears the mark of the English-born goldsmith, Anthony Nelme.

The reflector plate was sometimes made of looking glass. Only one set with London hall-marks is known to survive. These are in the collection of the Duke of Devonshire at Chatsworth and were made by John Boddington. There are numerous references in the eighteenth-century royal accounts[2] to the repair of these sconces, and fifteen looking glasses with silver sconces are referred to in a royal warrant dated as late as 22nd April 1799. Presumably these, with so much eighteenth-century royal plate, were melted to provide metal for the Prince Regent's Grand Service.

### Chandeliers

Silver chandeliers constitute one of the most extravagant uses of the metal; it is unlikely that many were ever made and even fewer have survived. The best known is that in the King's Presence Chamber at Hampton Court made for William III. This has twelve branches and is the work of the royal goldsmith, George Garthorne (Pl. 77). It is ornamented with the full range of

---

[1] Ill., E. A. Jones, *Windsor Castle Plate*, Pl. XXII.
[2] E. A. Jones, *Windsor Castle Plate*, p. xxvii.

decorative elements from the Huguenot stock, including interlacing strapwork, scalework, applied leaves, etc., and demonstrates
the virtuosity of the royal goldsmith. Two others, which according
to the 1721 inventory were at St. James's Palace, are now lost. A
few other examples exist, one at Chatsworth belonging to the
Duke of Devonshire and dating from the 1680's, another at
Drumlanrig Castle[1] in Scotland belonging to the Duke of Buccleuch, and a third, dating from about 1700, is at Knole.[2] The only
fully-marked chandelier recorded is the nine-branched one belonging to a private collector which was shown at the Toronto exhibition in 1958[3] This bears the London hall-mark for 1704 and the
maker's mark of John Boddington.

[1] This chandelier is said to have been given by Charles II as a wedding
present to his natural son, the Duke of Monmouth.
[2] Ill., Macquoid and Edwards, *Dictionary of English Furniture*, 2nd ed.,
1954, Vol. I, p. 328, Fig. 5.
[3] Cat. no. F3.

# CHAPTER VI

# Engraving on Silver

Engraved ornament, other than the heraldic bearings of owners, had been out of fashion in England[1] for several decades before 1688, as long, that is, as embossed ornament had been accepted as the appropriate decoration for plate. The revival of engraved ornament took place independently of the Huguenots, but was due in part at least to French influence, and the Huguenots were certainly closely connected with its development and florescence during this period. The engraved decoration of silver reached at this time a standard higher than had been known before. The practice of enclosing the owner's coat of arms within an elaborate Baroque cartouche gave the engraver a greater opportunity to display his skill than at any other time in the history of English silver. The first book of engraved ornament for the use of goldsmiths to appear in England was a reprint of one of the many sets of frieze designs by the French engraver, Jean Lepautre. It was entitled 'A New Booke of Fries Work Inv.<sup>t</sup> by J. le Pautre' and was published in London in 1676 by a certain John Overton. Another pattern book of which an English reprint appeared was the *Livre de Divers Ornements d'orfèvrerie* by Jean Mussard, engraved by J. L. Durant and first published in Geneva in 1673. The English version was entitled *A Book of Divers Ornaments proper for most sorts of Artificers, but particularly for such who engrave on Plate*. It was followed by a *New Book of Ornaments: Leaves, Frize-work, etc.* a reprint of another of J. L. Durant's books of engraved ornament. Although published in the 1670's, these

---

[1] With the exception of pieces engraved with commemorative subjects, such as the group of tankards believed to have been given by Sir Edmund Berry Godfrey to his friends after he had been knighted for his services during the Great Plague and the Fire of London (*Corporation Plate*, 1952, no. 66). Engraved floral ornament also appears on a group of tankards, modelled on a Scandinavian prototype, made in York.

pattern books would have remained in use well into the period covered by this book. They were, however, used more by the decorator of snuff-boxes and watch-cases than by the decorator of plate, as were the two publications of the immigrant Huguenot artist, Simon Gribelin, which are described below.

At about the same time that engraved ornament returned to fashion, the flat-chasing which had accompanied the earlier embossed ornament lost favour. The heavier metal used by the silversmiths of the last years of the seventeenth century was less suited to the process of chasing, and in any case, the taste of the period called for higher relief than could easily be achieved by flat-chasing. Nevertheless, one of the most remarkable examples of flat-chased work on English silver is found on the pair of octagonal dishes of 1698 by Benjamin Pyne in the Victoria and Albert Museum (Pl. 61). The borders are decorated with putti amongst foliage in flat-chasing while the coat of arms and cartouche in the centre of the dishes are engraved. Benjamin Pyne, though of English origin, is one of the silversmiths who is thought to have employed Huguenot craftsmen in his workshop, and the ornament of the dishes, which is derived from the English reprint of Jean Lepautre's book of frieze-work, is probably the work of a Huguenot.

The chinoiserie ornament which had been so popular for a brief period during the reigns of Charles II and James II, had been executed in flat-chasing, and as this technique went out of favour, so at the same time did the chinoiseries. During the 1680's and 1690's we find an alternative to the latter in a very attractive form of engraved ornament with human figures or animals amidst scrolling strawberry leaves, blossom and fruit. This ornament was more freely executed than the rigidly symmetrical designs of the early eighteenth century derived from French sources and seems to be of English origin. Thus while the later engraved designs can be traced back to the pattern books of ornament, these earlier ones are less repetitive and seem to spring from the fantasy of the engraver (Pl. 17B). Strawberry leaf ornament was not by any means confined to silver but is found about the same time on door and gun locks, on pistol and gun barrels and on snuff-boxes, that is on objects of brass, iron and steel. This style of engraving, though remote from the chinoiseries in derivation, had something of their gaiety and proved an effective substitute. The attractive engraving on a small salver in the parish church of Durrington, Wiltshire, of

1691, by Benjamin Pyne, consisting of a cherub, birds, a lion and a lamb amongst flowers and foliage is quite unusual in that it is executed in a very fine version of the 'wriggle-work' which is usually confined to engraving on pewter.[1] A mug with London hall-mark for 1692 and maker's mark I.C. is engraved in the same manner with boys and birds amongst flowers and foliage, probably by the same artist (Pl. 16A).

This native English engraved ornament was too informal in character for the Huguenot vessel forms and it was soon replaced by a style closer to that current in France. The origin of the Huguenot decoration can be found in the vast number of sheets of engraved ornament issued by the three great masters of French late Baroque, Jean Lepautre (1618–82), Jean Berain (1637–1711) and Paul Ducerceau (*c.* 1630–1713). The main elements of their ornament were acanthus foliage, strapwork, scale ornament and figures in symmetrical arrangement. The French style with all its profusion of ornament can best be seen in the pattern book of Sieur de Masson, *Nouveaux desseins pour graver sur l'orfèvrerie.* Whereas in France elaborate engraved ornament was applied to a variety of objects, including teapots, coffee-pots and cups, écuelles, dishes and saucers, in England it was confined to salvers, casters, beakers, tea-caddies, snuff and toilet boxes, knives, forks and spoons. On other pieces it is rare to find much engraved ornament beyond the cartouche enclosing the owner's or donor's coat of of arms and even this was often of the simplest design. Where elaborate ornament was required it usually took the form of cast and applied work, at any rate on the larger pieces of plate.

The vast majority of the engravers on silver are anonymous. Not only did they rarely sign their work, but with very few exceptions we have no record of their names, although in many cases it is their work that has transformed a simple piece of plate into a work of art. Some of the engraved ornament on silver of this period is of so elaborate a character that it can claim consideration as a work of art in its own right. While the ordinary heraldic engraver would not have thought of adding his own initials or signature to a coat of arms, these more ambitious pieces were sometimes signed. As a result of the discovery of such signatures and the chance survival of other sources of evidence, we are able to give some account of three engravers of our period. Before dealing with these, mention

[1] *Silver Treasures from English Churches*, 1955, no. 137.

should be made of a certain L. King whose signature accompanies the engraved cartouches enclosing the arms of the donor and of the college on a ewer and basin of 1685 and also on a two-handled cup of 1689 at St. John's College,[1] Oxford. Another artist is known by his initials and by only one piece, but this one of the greatest splendour; namely the silver table presented to William III by the City of London. The whole of the top is superbly decorated with heraldic engraving signed with the initials R.H.S. (Pl. 84). In view of the importance of the commission and the magnificence of the table, the artist must have been one of the leading London copperplate engravers of his day. Of comparable quality is the table-top engraved with the arms and cipher of the first Duke of Devonshire. This is now mounted in a later frame. The engraving is signed 'B. Gentot in. fecit', evidently for the French engraver, Blaize Gentot, who was born in Lyons in 1658 and was working in Paris in 1700. Gentot was, incidentally, the engraver of the copperplates of Jean Tijou's pattern book of ironwork, entitled *Nouveau Livre de Serrurerie*, published in Paris in 1693. As Tijou was employed at the first Duke's seat at Chatsworth during the late 1680's, it was presumably through him that Gentot obtained the commission to engrave the table-top. Whether he did the work in England or in France is not known.

The first engraver of whose biography anything is known is Simon Gribelin, who came from a well-known Huguenot family in Blois. He was born there in 1661 and, according to Horace Walpole's *Catalogue of Engravers*, he came to London about 1680 along with the first wave of immigrants from France. He became a member of the Clockmakers' Company of London in 1686, perhaps because of the resistance offered by the Goldsmiths' Company, perhaps merely because much of his work consisted of engraving watch-cases for members of that Company. His first published book of designs, entitled *A Book of Ornaments useful to Jewellers, watchmakers & all other Artists*, which appeared in 1697 (Pl. 91A), consisted of designs intended for the decoration of watch-cocks, watch-cases and snuff-boxes, but his second publication, issued in 1700, was aimed, according to the text of the title-page (Pl. 90), at a wider public. It was entitled *A Book of Ornaments usefull to all Artists*. In both cases his designs were based on the familiar classical acanthus ornament of the Louis XIV period.

[1] Ill., H. C. Moffatt, *Old Oxford Plate*, Pls. LXXXIV, LXXXV.

His first book did not appear until 1697, but he was doubtless employed by his fellow Huguenots before that date. The usual practice amongst engravers of ornament such as Gribelin seems to have been to keep copies or pulls of the engraved work they executed and, when a sufficient number and variety of designs had been collected, to issue them in the form of a pattern book for the guidance of other artists. It follows that such pattern books, far from containing new material, as their title pages usually claim, often included designs that had been executed many years before the issue of the book and were, in consequence, no longer fashionable.

The engravers upon silver can be divided into two main classes. Firstly, those who relied entirely for their living on engraving plate, watch-cases and book-plates, mostly that is to say, heraldic work; and secondly the engraver-illustrators, who, besides producing prints for collectors and illustrating books, were prepared to decorate an important piece of silver for a fee. Neither of these two classes worked in the goldsmiths' shop; only the simplest engraved borders are likely to have been executed by the goldsmith himself, and any work calling for a higher degree of skill was put out to a specialist.

Gribelin belonged to the second class of engraver; far from confining himself to silver, he illustrated books and issued a series of engravings after old master paintings in the English collections. Walpole thought little of his work, and dismissed him with the comment 'His works have no more merit than finicalness, and that not in perfection, can give them'. Walpole qualified this severe judgement, however, subsequently: 'He executed a great number of small plates on gold, silver and copper; chiefly for books, but was fittest to engrave patterns for goldsmith's work.' He also relates: 'I have a thick quarto collected by himself, of all his small plates. which was sold by his son after his decease; which happened, without any previous sickness in Long Acre. He caught cold by going to see the king in the house of lords; fell ill that night, continued so the next day, and died the third, aged 72.'

Through the survival in the British Museum of his book of prints, perhaps the one referred to by Walpole, which is entitled *Livre d'Estampes de Sim. Gribelin, fait Relié a Londre* 1722, we are well-informed concerning his œuvre. This book contains a selection of his work: prints, proofs taken from engraved silver and also counter-proofs. A proof taken from a piece of engraved silver shows the subject and lettering, if any, in reverse; in a counter-proof, an impression was taken from the engraving, and, while the ink on this impression was still wet, it was in turn printed on another piece of paper, thus producing an impression in the same sense as the original engraving.

There are a number of pulls taken from engraved snuff-box lids, but the most interesting prints in the collection from our point of view are the series of engraved salvers, or tables as they were then known. A number of these salvers still exist but Gribelin's finest surviving work is the oval dish illustrated in Pl. 88. Though unsigned, the engraving is recognizably from his hand. His manner was, of course, copied by lesser engravers and the tea-caddy in Pl. 46A illustrates engraved ornament based on his designs but not executed by him.

A considerable number of the finely engraved salvers surviving from this period owe their origin to a custom dating back to the sixteenth century, namely for the Officer of State responsible for the Great Seal, or other seals of office, to retain as a perquisite the discarded silver matrix when such a seal became obsolete through the death of the Sovereign or a change in his title, and to have the metal of which it was composed made into one or more pieces of plate. In the earlier seventeenth century, the piece of plate took the form of a cup, but, during the reign of William III, it became more usual to have a salver made, the top of which was then engraved with a representation of the seal from the matrix of which it had been formed. The earliest of these salvers now known to survive is that made from the Lord Chancellor's seal of Charles Montagu, Earl of Halifax. The seal had to be renewed in 1694 on the death of William III's consort, Mary. The salver made from this seal matrix was engraved by Simon Gribelin and a pull from it is in Gribelin's album. The salver itself is now in the Burrell Collection at Glasgow (Pl. 92). For some reason which cannot at present be explained, a replica of this salver was made by David Willaume junior in 1726, nine years after the death of the Earl of Halifax. This second salver has also survived and is now in the Schiller Collection at the Inner Temple. Two other extant salvers made from seal matrices were executed for Henry Boyle, who was Chancellor of the Irish Exchequer from 1701 to 1708. He received the first on the death of William III in 1702 and the second on the

Act of Union with Scotland in 1707. Both of these salvers are now the property of the Chatsworth Trustees and pulls from them are to be found in Gribelin's album (Pl. 91B). Another salver, made, however, after the death of Gribelin, belongs to the Corporation of Kingston-upon-Thames and was made from the Great Seal of Queen Caroline, George II's consort. It dates from 1738 and was made by Henry Herbert.[1]

The salvers engraved by Gribelin (Pls. 91B, 92) must be reckoned amongst the finest pieces of engraved English plate in existence and rival in quality even the most famous of all the seal salvers, that made by Paul de Lamerie in 1727 from the Chancellor's seal of Sir Robert Walpole (Pl. 94), (see below, p. 75).

Amongst the cups made from seals at this period is one belonging to the Corporation of Newcastle-upon-Tyne,[2] which is inscribed 'The last Privey Seale wch belonged to England before the Union of Great Brittaine wch tooke place the first of May 1707'. The cup is unmarked but bears the crest of John Holles, Duke of Newcastle, appointed Lord Privy Seal in 1705. A replica[3] of this cup, also unmarked, but known to have been made in 1708 by a certain John Coggs for the Duke of Newcastle, whose crest it bears, is in the collection of the Duke of Portland. The engraving on such cups does not, however, compare with that on the salvers executed by Gribelin and was probably left to an ordinary heraldic engraver. Gribelin also engraved a number of salvers with owners' arms, and proofs from four such salvers are included in his book. The arrangement of the engraved designs on the seal salvers has been borrowed by Gribelin on a pair of ewers and basins presented to St. John's College, Cambridge by Thomas Wentworth of Wentworth Woodhouse.[4] They bear the London hall-mark for 1717 and maker's mark of the London goldsmith, Samuel Wastell. The engraving shows every sign of being Gribelin's work. His book of engravings also includes a number of large coats of arms with mantling, evidently intended for salvers.

Another engraver of silver plate of this period of whom something is known is Benjamin Rhodes;[5] our knowledge of him

[1] Ill., Cat., *Corporation Plate*, 1952, Pl. XXXV, no. 129.
[2] *Corporation Plate*, 1952, no. 102.
[3] Ill., E. A. Jones, *Welbeck Plate*, Pl. III.
[4] Ill., E. A. Jones, *Cambridge Plate*, Pl. XC.
[5] For a fuller treatment of his work, see *Apollo*, Vol. LXV, May 1957, ps. 173–176, Charles Oman, 'English Engravers on Plate. I—Benjamin Rhodes'.

and his work is due to the chance survival of his account book amongst the papers of Hoare's Bank, his former employers. The account book covers the period from 1st January 1694 to 6th January 1698, only a very brief period of his working life. Rhodes was one of the lesser breeds of engraver and was mostly occupied with the more or less mechanical repetition of heraldic crests or coats of arms on all kinds of plate. Like Gribelin he produced a pattern book, but of a less ambitious kind. Entitled *A New Book of Cyphers* and published in 1723, it provided a large number of designs of typical early eighteenth-century character (Pl. 89A). In spite of his claim in the title that they were new designs, they evidently constituted the stock patterns which he had been using for many years before the date of publication. The account book shows a rough sketch of each coat of arms he was required to engrave, and in some cases a counter-proof of the actual engraving. It also shows the prices he charged for his work. The coat of arms of the Duke of St. Albans, of which he includes a counter-proof in his account book, is the most ambitious of his heraldic engravings and also the most highly paid; he received £1 for it (Pl. 89B). The heraldry on the cup and cover illustrated in Pl. 2, which was presented to Trinity College, Cambridge in 1697 by Henry Boyle, is also his work. He received the sum of 15s. 6d. for engraving two coats of arms and one crest upon it. From the fact that the pieces engraved by Rhodes which have been identified bear the marks of different goldsmiths, it is evident that Hoare, who was not a practising craftsman but a retailer and banker, gave out work to a number of working goldsmiths. Unlike the latter, who would not have been able to afford to keep a stock of plate, Hoare evidently kept such a stock and sent the pieces out to be engraved as soon as they had found a purchaser.

Unlike Simon Gribelin, Benjamin Rhodes did not sign his work; his status as an engraver is illustrated by this fact. His employer, Sir Richard Hoare, would doubtless have considered it presumptuous on his part had he done so. A third engraver on silver, again of higher status than Rhodes, was Joseph Simpson or Sympson, who engraved and signed two very fine salvers which are still extant. Like Rhodes, Simpson also produced a book of designs, entitled *A New Book of Cyphers*. Simpson is recorded in Horace Walpole's *Catalogue of Engravers* in the following terms 'Joseph Simpson was very low in his profession, cutting arms on pewter plates; till having studied at the academy, he was employed by Tillemans on a plate of Newmarket, to which he was permitted to put his name; and which, though it did not please the painter, served to make Simpson known'. In spite of Walpole's condemnation, Simpson was evidently highly regarded at the time, for one of the salvers[1] he engraved was made for the Chancellor of the Exchequer, Sir Robert Walpole, out of the first Exchequer seal of George I. Apart from the usual representations of the seal itself, it is engraved with Phaeton and a figure of Victory flanked by captives and military trophies. It has no hall-mark but bears the maker's mark of William Lukin. The second signed salver by Simpson is now preserved in the Victoria and Albert Museum (Pl. 93). It also bears the maker's mark of William Lukin but is fully hall-marked for 1717. It is engraved with the arms of Richard, 5th Viscount Ingram impaling those of his wife, Lady Anne Howard. Like the other signed salvers, the artist has not been satisfied with heraldry alone, but has enclosed the arms within an elaborate frame composed of figures emblematic of the elements while below is a small battle piece. The only other signed pieces known are the ewer and basin of 1715, also by William Lukin, in the collection of the Duke of Devonshire at Chatsworth, but others will probably be recognized in the future.

A far more noteworthy artist than either Gribelin or Simpson was occupied, at any rate during part of our period, with engraving plate. This was William Hogarth, who in 1712 was bound apprentice to the goldsmith Ellis Gamble, under whose instruction he learnt to engrave plate. His period of apprenticeship expired in 1717/18 and he then set up as an engraver of coats of arms, presumably on plate or for book-plates, and of trade-cards, shop-bills and frontispieces. His earliest recorded engraving, which bears his initials and is dated 1716, appears to have been executed on a salver and depicts a scene from the *Rape of the Lock* (Pl. 96). From about the same time is the trade-card of his employer, Ellis Gamble (Pl. 95). A third early work is his own trade-card, which is inscribed W. Hogarth and dated 23rd April 1720.[2] John Nichols, in his *Biographical Anecdotes of William Hogarth*, lists amongst his engraved works a 'large Coat of Arms with Terms of the Four

[1] Ill., *Apollo*, Vol. LXV, July 1957, Charles Oman, 'English Engravers on Plate. III—Joseph Sympson and William Hogarth', Fig. I, p. 286.
[2] Ill., R. B. Beckett, *Hogarth*, 1949, Pl. E. 1.

Seasons'. This is a rendering of the arms of Ayala, and is, in fact, also a proof taken from a large engraved salver, apparently no longer in existence. It is not known how long Hogarth continued to accept commissions to engrave silver plate, but in view of his success in other directions it is improbable that he went on for long. Some evidence can be gathered from the *Anecdotes of William Hogarth, written by himself*, London, 1833, where it is stated (p. 2/3): 'It was therefore conformable to my own wishes that I was taken from school, and served long apprenticeship to a silver-plate engraver. I soon found this business in every respect too limited . . . and I determined that silver-plate engraving should be followed no longer than necessity obliged me to it. Engraving on copper was, at twenty years of age, my utmost ambition.' This would seem to indicate that he ceased engraving plate about 1718, when he completed his apprenticeship. In spite of the existence of the four engravings mentioned above, which date from the period when he was decorating silver, it is extremely difficult to attribute pieces of engraved silver to him. A certain type of elaborate late Baroque cartouche of the type seen in Pls. 8 and 64, is sometimes described as being in his manner. In fact, there is no reason to attribute such designs particularly to him. He would, like his contemporaries, have used the fashionable style of the period. The most convincing attribution of a piece of engraved silver to his hand is that of the second Great Seal salver of Sir Robert Walpole, now in the Victoria and Albert Museum (Pl. 94). This salver was made in 1728 by Paul de Lamerie, and the tradition that it was engraved by Hogarth goes back to 1781.[1] Whether Hogarth was still engraving silver as late as 1728 is open to question, but there can be no doubt that a commission from Paul de Lamerie, who was already one of the leading goldsmiths of London, to engrave a salver for the First Lord of the Treasury, was not one to be rejected as unworthy of his notice. The quality of the engraving on this salver is such that it is recognized as the finest in the whole group of seal salvers.

[1] John Nichols, *Biographical Anecdotes of William Hogarth*, 1781, p. 148. Amongst the list of engravings is 'The Great Seal of England with a distant view of London; an impression from a large silver table'. For a full discussion of this question see *Apollo*, loc. cit., ps. 286–289.

# CHAPTER VII

# The Cost of Plate

It has been mentioned above that the Huguenot practice of using cast rather than wrought plate consumed even larger quantities of metal than had previously been the case. There had been an extravagant use of silver ever since the Restoration: huge wine-coolers and wine fountains had been made not only for the great families but for the lesser nobility, and silver furniture was no longer confined to royal palaces. Even Samuel Pepys had a silver table. This lavish use of silver continued during the period dealt with here. The following extract[1] from an account of the Earl of Devonshire with Messrs. Child and Rogers, Goldsmiths, Temple Bar, in 1687 gives some idea of the quantities of plate that were ordered by the nobility at the beginning of the period:

|  | £ | s. | d. |
|---|---|---|---|
| for a great silver cistern, weight 3,496 oz., at 7s. per oz. | 1223 | 12 | 0 |
| for a case | 6 | 10 | 0 |
| for a sugar box, weighing 32 oz., at 7s. per oz. | 11 | 3 | 3 |
| for graving a bason and ewer | 1 | 15 | 0 |
| for boiling the plate, which I sold at 5s. 8d. per oz. | 1 | 0 | 0 |
| for a great jar, 2 flower pots, 4 little jars, a bottle with a spoon, weight 255½ oz. at 6s. per oz. | 76 | 13 | 0 |
| for a pair of andirons, 143 oz. 12 dwt., at 7s. 2d. per oz. | 51 | 9 | 0 |
| for the iron work | 0 | 12 | 0 |
| for 2 figures on pedestals, 164 oz. 10 dwt. at 6s. 8d. per oz. | 49 | 7 | 0 |
| for 2 branch candlesticks 172 oz. 14 dwt. at 6s. per oz. | 51 | 16 | 0 |

[1] W. Chaffers, *Gilda Aurifabrorum*, p. 240.

for 1 dozen and ½ of silver gilt plates, 475 oz.,  £   s.   d.

    at 8s. 6d. per oz. is  201  17   6

a total of approximately 4,740 oz. of plate.

A nobleman of this period acquired plate not only for use but also to enable him to keep up the state appropriate to his rank and dignity. The records kept by John Hervey, first Earl of Bristol,[1] which cover the whole period of this book, give a full picture of the purchases of plate of a nobleman, who, although wealthy, was by no means one of the richest of his time. In the period between 1688 and 1727 he spent £6,027 4s. 3d. on plate, a figure which would have been considerably larger but for the fact that he traded in a quantity of unfashionable plate when ordering new pieces. In all the old plate melted and re-fashioned at his order amounted to 2,164 ounces. In one year, 1696, the Earl spent no less than £649 2s. 11d. on plate. His purchases in the period 1688–1727 included 6 pairs of silver andirons, 12 large silver sconces, 10 silver frames for glass sconces, 2 silver cisterns, one of which he passed on to his eldest son, a large basin and ewer, a monteith, 38 dishes of various sizes and 6 dozen of silver plates. Although he had so much of his father's plate melted and refashioned, the Earl did not hesitate to purchase second-hand plate at the auction sales. In this he was no exception. Thus the huge wine cistern and fountain bought for George II when Prince of Wales, was originally made for the Earl of Meath. Of the series of great wine cisterns acquired by Catherine the Great of Russia and now at the Hermitage Museum, two still bear the arms of their former owners, the Earl of Scarsdale and the Duke of Kingston respectively. The wine cistern which Hervey bought from Messrs. Duncombe and Pigeon, executors of Mr. Baptist May, is still preserved at Ickworth and was 17 years old when he got it, for it bears the mark of the London goldsmith, Robert Cooper, and the London hallmark for 1680. It is a highly embossed piece[2] in a taste which must by 1697 have seemed rather coarse.

There are many references to purchases from the Huguenot goldsmiths in the Earl's accounts; he patronized Pierre Harache in 1699, Pierre Platel in 1709, Louis Cuny in 1714 and David Willaume on repeated occasions between 1699 and 1727. It is

---

[1] *The Diary of John Hervey, first Earl of Bristol*, Wells 1894, ps. 136–54.
[2] Ill., Cat., *Exhibition of Treasures from National Trust Houses*, London 1958, Pl. X, no. 151.

interesting to note that whereas he dealt directly with the Huguenot goldsmiths, whom he refers to as French in the accounts, his other purchases seem to have been made from the banker-goldsmiths who put out their work to plate-workers.

The prices he paid for plate show much variation. The actual cost per ounce of the metal was fixed by the Mint, but the goldsmith was free to make his own charge for working up the plate (i.e. for fashion). In 1695 two dishes cost the Earl 5s. 2d. per ounce plus 4s. per ounce for fashion. In 1703 he paid 10d. per ounce fashion for a set of plates and dishes. The two French firedogs which he bought second-hand in 1703 cost 5s. 5d. per ounce for the metal and only 1d. per ounce was reckoned for fashion. Much higher prices were sometimes paid: thus a pair of branch candlesticks and a pair of gilt sconces cost 7s. 6d. per ounce from Mr. Richard Hoare in 1696. In this case, however, the higher price was probably due to the additional cost of gilding the pieces. The Duke of Devonshire had paid Mr. Child 8s. 6d. per ounce for gilt plate in 1687. An interesting indication of the reputation of the leading Huguenot goldsmiths can be gathered from Hervey's note relating to a purchase he made in 1709 from Pierre Platel to the effect that he had paid 'more than the office allowed', presumably in order to secure the services of this prominent goldsmith. This fact contrasts curiously with the grievance of the London goldsmiths in their petition of 1711, when it was claimed that the necessitous strangers 'whose desperate fortunes obliged them to work at miserable rates' were responsible for the decline in the fortunes of the former. The Jewel Office papers in the Public Record Office[1] give us some information upon the cost of plate at the close of our period. In 1727 the Treasury noted in a Minute to the Jewel Office that ambassadors and other officials of state who were entitled to receive allowances of plate from the Jewel Office were having vessels of elaborate design made and thus considerably increasing the cost of plate to the state. The Master of the Jewel Office pointed out in his reply that ambassadors were entitled to receive plate made to whatever fashion they might choose and that no limit had ever been fixed to the cost of fashion. The cost to the Exchequer had averaged between £2,900 and £3,000 for each ambassador. He suggested that the example of the then Lord Chancellor should be recognized as a standard. This official

[1] L.C. 5/114.

had received 4,000 ounces of white plate under the sign manual of George I and the cost including fashion had been £1,700, that is to say, 8s. 6d. per ounce. The plate in question had been of plain design and the Master of the Jewel Office commented: 'I fear (this) will be found too strait an allowance in most cases especially that of ambassadors who I believe will not be contented as his Lordship has been to receive the better part of his warrant in common plate and dishes.' It will be seen that prices of plate had risen considerably since the end of the seventeenth century when the Duke of Devonshire was paying between 6s. and 8s. per ounce, inclusive of fashion, to a leading London goldsmith. From the same Jewel Office papers we learn that the cost of re-gilding just under 1,300 ounces of store plate for the coronation festivities of George II in 1727 was £2,038 2s. 4d.; that is, approximately 3s. 2d. per ounce.

After the death of the poet, Matthew Prior, in 1721, his silver plate was offered for sale to Robert Harley, Earl of Oxford, and a list of the pieces he purchased with weights and prices paid is preserved amongst the papers at Welbeck Abbey. This list shows that prices averaged about 5s. per ounce, sometimes a little more, sometimes slightly less, with little regard to the type of plate concerned. The lowness of these prices can doubtless be explained by the fact that the plate was second-hand and was, therefore, reckoned at about its bare bullion value.

| | | £ | s. | d. |
|---|---|---|---|---|
| NEW STERLING | | | | |
| 2 great wrought Silver Sconces, at 5s. 5d. per ounce................... 90 oz. | | 24 | 7 | 6 |
| OLD STERLING | | | | |
| 1 great Candlestick with three branches, at 5s. 2d................ 69.10 dwt. | | 17 | 19 | 1 |
| 4 ditto, without branches............ 128.15 ,, | | 33 | 5 | 2½ |
| 3 large Candlesticks with branches 128.12 ,, | | 33 | 4 | 5 |
| 2 lesser Ditto ........................ 40 ,, | | 10 | 6 | 8 |
| Snuffers and Pan..................... 14.4 ,, | | 3 | 13 | 4 |
| 1 Table Standish with a Bell Sand Box & Ink Box..................... 80 ,, | | 20 | 13 | 4 |
| One Sand Box, Ink Box and Wafer Box ................................. 40.15 ,, | | 10 | 10 | 6½ |
| One large Water Pott with a Lid 37.4 ,, | | 9 | 12 | 2½ |
| Two large Scallop Shel Dishes ... 26.1 ,, | | 6 | 14 | 7 |

|  |  |  | £ | s. | d. |
|---|---|---|---|---|---|
| Two round Sallad Dishes ......... | 34 | ,, | 8 | 15 | 8 |
| A Mustard Cup with a Lid and Spoon ............................. | 9.4 | ,, | 2 | 7 | 6 |
| Two large Soupe Spoons............ | 16.18 | ,, | 4 | 7 | 4 |
| One Marrow Spoon.................. | 2.10 | ,, |  | 12 | 11 |
| 12 Tea Spoons or Sweetmeat Spoons.............................. | 11.15 | ,, | 3 | 0 | 8½ |
| 35 Table Spoons.................... | 103 | ,, | 26 | 12 | 2 |
| 6 ditto at Downe-Hall ........... | 17.19 | ,, | 4 | 12 | 7 |
| 36 Table Forks ..................... | 105 | ,, | 27 | 2 | 6 |
| 6 ditto at Downe-Hall.............. | 17.5 | ,, | 4 | 9 |  |
| 30 Knives Silver hafts (6 whereof at Down Hall ................. | 75.0 | ,, | 19 | 7 | 6 |
|  |  |  | 271 | 14 | 9 |

# APPENDIX

# Entries relating to purchases of silver, extracted from the diaries of John Hervey, first Earl of Bristol, 1688–1727

1688

Oct. 4.  Paid for a silver hanging candlestick for the nursery, weighing 17 ounces, 10 pennyweight. £5.11.0

1699

Jan. 24  Paid for a pair of silver andirons for my dear wife her closet chimney. £13.5.0

Dec. 19  Paid Mrs. Harache for a silver standish £15.10.0

1693

Feb. 9  Paid Mr. Robert ffowle in full for a pair of large andirons and a silver pair of scales. £88.5.6

1695

May 18  Paid Mr. James Seamer the goldsmith for 2 table stands £15

June 12  Paid Mr. Ed. Waldegrave the goldsmith for a bason and ewer, weighing 244 ounces and a half, at 5s. 3d. per ounce £63.3.2.

June 23  Paid Mr. Chambers and Partner in full of their bill for the silver stand and salvers etc. £30

Oct. 7  Paid Mr. James Seamers the goldsmiths man Thomas Outlaw for the great silver chased basket, weighing 128 ounces, 4 dwt. at 5s. 3d. per ounce £34.10.0

Oct. 17  Paid Mr. James Seamer for a monteith weight 75 ounces at 5s. 4d. per ounce and a chafing dish weight 24 ounces 15 dwt. at 6s. 6d. per ounce, together £28.50.

Nov. 5  Paid Mr. Richard Hoar the goldsmith for a pair of

branch candlesticks weighing 78 ounces 2 dwt. and for a pair of gilt sconces weighing 46 ounces 14 dwt., both at 7s. 6d. per ounce £46.15.6

Nov. 7    Paid Mr. Edw. Waldegrave, a goldsmith in Russel street, for 11 dishes, 1 dozen of plates, a coffee pot, & a porrige ladle, weighing 802 ounces, at 5s. 3¼ per ounce, & for the graving £211.7.0, £7.3.0 in money, the rest in old plate of my dear fathers.

Nov. 19   For 2 dishes made by Mr. Chambers weighing 154½ ounces at 4d. per ounce fashion, & 10 shillings for graving them, & the plate at 5s. 2d. per ounce £42.19.9  Gave him the weight in old plate.

1697

May 7    Paid mr. Duncombe & Mr. Pigeon (as executors of Mr. Baptist May) for a large silver cistern, 2 dozen of nurled plates, 1 large cup & cover, 1 basin, 1 chamber pot, 1 ladle, & 1 skimmer, all weighing 1128 ounces 15 pennyweight, which at 5s. 4d. per ounce come to £301

Dec. 7    Paid Mr. Chambers his bill in full for a Tea-kettle & lamp, weight 90 ounces 11 dwt. at 6s. 2d. & for a chafing dish with a cawdle heater, weight 51 ounces 18 dwt. at 5s. 5d. per ounce, in all £42.19.0.

Dec. 31.   Paid Watt Compton goldsmith in Lincolns Inn Fields for 2 pair of Andirons & 2 little knobs for tongs and shovel weighing 307 ounces 14 dwt. at 5s. 4d per ounce £82.1.0.

1699

Jan. 17   Paid David Willaume for the silver borders of 8 glass sconces for the drawing room weighing 231 ounces 13 dwt. £75.5.0

Jan. 20   Paid ditto for a pair of the same borders for the chimney weighing 53 ounces 13 dwt. at 6s. 6d. & for a pair of chimney sconces all of silver weighing 90 ounces 3 dwt. at 7 shillings per ounces, in all £47.6.0

Feb. 21   Paid David Willaume for the 8 great silver sconces weighing 491 ounces at 7s. shilling per ounce & for graving etc. in all £175.

1700

Jan. 27 — Paid George Lewis, silversmith, for 2 pair of plate andirons being French plate at 5s. 5d. per ounce intrinsic value & 1d. fashion in all 5s. 6d. per ounce, the large pair weighed 135 ounces 2 dwt.: the dogs 28 ounces 9 dwt. so cost £45

July 6 — Paid Willaume the French silversmith for 2 pottage & 4 ragout spoons £15.15.0

Oct. 26 — Paid Lanseter for 2 silver jars etc. delivered Bury fair 1699, £3.9.0

1703

June 23 — Paid Mr. Chambers & Comp. in full of their bill for new plate (besides 1236 ounces they had of me in old plate) £20.16.0 The 22 new dishes & 3 dozen of plates weighed in all 1668 ounces 5 dwt. at 10 pence for fashion.

1707

Dec. 17 — Paid Mr. Chambers for the two new pair of candlesticks & for a dressing weight for dear wife etc. £20.10.0

1708

March 9 — Paid Mr. Thomas Brydon for a pair of candlesticks, snuffers & stand which I made a present of to Monsieur Masson £16.13.6

Dec. 2 — Paid Mr. Chambers for a great silver nurled dish etc. in full £18.15.7

1709

Jan. 11 — Paid Pierre Platel the French silver smith, more than the office allowed for Nanns silver frame & the 5 covers to it £63.10.0

1714

Oct. 19 — Paid Louis Cuny for my Earls Coronet £14

1716

Aug. 29 — Paid Mr. Chambers for a silver stew-pan weighing 67 ounces 14 dwt. & for a silver chamber pot weighing 30 ounces, both at 6s. 6d. per ounce, & for graving them etc., in all £32.7.3

[83]

1727

April 17    Paid David Willaume the silversmith for the case of 12 gilt knives, 12 spoons & 12 forks, weighing 131 ounces at 5s. 8½d. bought at the D. of Shrewsburys sale, & for boiling & mending old plate, in all £37.10.0

April 23    Paid & allowed for the several pieces of plate I bought which were Lady Effinghams, (besides the cistern of £82.11.0 I gave my son Lord Hervey & charged before) in all £58.4.0., which I made the whole I was chargeable for £140.15.0

# BIBLIOGRAPHY OF WORKS REFERRED TO IN THE NOTES

William Chaffers: *Gilda Auri fabrorum: a history of London gold-smiths and plate-workers and their marks stamped on plate*, 1883.

Joan Evans: 'Huguenot goldsmiths in England and Ireland', 1933, (Reprinted from the *Proceedings of the Huguenot Society of London*, XIV).

E. Alfred Jones: *The Old English Plate of the Emperor of Russia*, 1909; *The Old Plate of the Cambridge Colleges*, 1910; *The Gold and Silver of Windsor Castle*, 1911; *Catalogue of the Collection of Old Plate of William Francis Farrer at No. 7 St. James's Square, London*, 1924; *Catalogue of Plate belonging to the Duke of Portland, K.G., G.C.V.O., at Welbeck Abbey*, 1935.

*The Diary of John Hervey, 1st Earl of Bristol*, Wells 1894.

G. Bernard Hughes: *Small Antique Silverware*, 1957.

H. C. Moffatt: *Old Oxford Plate*, 1906.

*Œuvres de Bijouterie et Joaillerie des XVII<sup>e</sup> et XVIII<sup>e</sup> Siècles*, Paris, n.d.

Philip A. S. Phillips: *Paul de Lamerie, A Study of his Life and Work*, 1935.

Walter S. Prideaux: *Memorials of the Goldsmiths' Company*, 1335–1815, 2 vols., 1896–97.

Gerald Taylor: *Silver; an illustrated introduction to British plate from the Middle Ages to the present day*, 1956.

# EXHIBITIONS REFERRED TO IN THE NOTES

Messrs. Christie, Manson & Woods: *Silver Treasures from English Churches*, 1955; *Treasures from National Trust Houses*, 1958.

Worshipful Company of Goldsmiths, Goldsmiths' Hall: *Historic Plate of the City of London*, 1951; *Corporation Plate of England and Wales*, 1952.

Royal Academy: *English Taste in the 18th century; Winter Exhibition*, 1955–56.

Royal Ontario Museum, Toronto: *Seven centuries of English Domestic Silver*, 1958.

Victoria and Albert Museum: *Works of Art belonging to the Livery Companies of the City of London*, 1926.

# Index

Andirons, 59, 60, 61, 62, 63, 64, Pl. 85B
Aparn, 54, 55
Archambo, Peter, 9, 22, 27
Assay cups, 58

Barnard, John, 63, Pl. 71A
Basins, 4, 10, 43, 44, 45, Frontispiece, Pls. 38, 62, 63, 64
Bathurst, Benjamin, 32
Bently, Benjamin, 57
Berain, Jean, 5, 68
Bird, Joseph, 55, Pl. 73B
Blackford, Anthony, Pl. 76A
Boddington, John, 20, 31, 48, 64, 65, Pls. 2, 15B
Boyle, Henry, 73, Pls. 2, 91B
Bread baskets, 54, 55, Pl. 58B
Britannia Standard, 26, 27, 28, 57 (Provincial Offices Act), 27
Brunswick, Duke of, 10, 35, Pls. 23, 27
Brydon, Thomas, 57, Pls. 75B, 76B

Caddinets, 58
Candelabra, 56, 57
Candlestands (torchères), 59, 60
Candlesticks, 55, 56, Pls. 73A, B, C, 74A, B
Casters, 50, 52, 53, 54, 68, Pls. 78A, B, 79B
Catherine, Empress of Russia, 11, 51, 77, Pl. 65A
Chamber candlesticks, 56, Pl. 70B
Chamber-pots, 45
Chandeliers, 59, 64, 65, Pl. 77
Charnelhouse, William, 20, 46
Chartier, John, 9, 33, 40, Pls. 3, 17A
Child and Rogers, Messrs., 76
Clausen, Nicholas, 60, Pl. 87
Coffee-beakers and cups, 8, 68
Coffee and chocolate-pots, 28, 47, 48, 68, Pls. 49A, B, 50A, B, 51A, B, 52A, B, 53
Coggs, John, 72

Cooper, Matthew, 51, Pl. 66B
  Robert, 58, 77, Pl. 83*b*
Cooqus, John, 16
Corbet, Thomas, 47, Pl. 50B
Cornock, Edward, 58, Pl. 83*c*
Courtauld, Augustine, 10, 27, 42
Crespin, Paul, 9, 11
Cruet frames, 54, Pls. 80A, B
Cumberland Plate, 10, Pls. 23, 27
Cuny, Louis, 27, 32, 77, 83, Pls. 4, 40B, 68A, 70B

Denny, W. and Backe, John, 55, Pl. 73C
Devonshire, Duke of, 38, 44, 50, 60, 65, 69, Frontispiece
Dinner service, 50, 55
Dish covers, 58
Downes, John, 39, Pl. 13B
Dragonnades, 13, 14 n.
Dubois, John, 16
Ducerceau, Paul, 5, 68
Durant, J. L., 66

Écuelles, 8, 55, 68, Pls. 69A, B
Edwards, John, 53, Pl. 78A
Epergnes, 54, 55
Evelyn, John, 14
Ewers, 10, 33, 43, 44, 45, 50, Frontispiece, Pls. 30A, 31, 34A, B, 38

Farrell, John, 48, Pl. 46B
Fawdery, John, 20, 24, 64, Pl. 71B
  William, 20, 41, 47, Pls. 30B, 52A
Feline, Edward, 27
Field cups and covers, 58
Fireplace furniture, 59, 62
Flagons, 40, Pl. 11
Fleming, William, 48, Pl. 57A
Folkingham, Thomas, 48, 54, Pls. 48A, 58B
Footstool, 60, Pl. 87
Fraillon, James, 10, 56, 58, Pls. 74B, 82A
Fruit bowls, 50

# Plates

1. *Standing cup. Benjamin Pyne, 1705. Pewterers' Company. H. 22½ in.*

2. *Two-handled cup. John Boddington, 1697.*
*Engraved by Benjamin Rhodes. Trinity College, Cambridge.*

3. *Two-handled cup. John Chartier, 1699. Ashmolean Museum. H. 9½ in.*

4. *Two-handled cup. Louis Cuny, 1702. Private Collection. H. $9\frac{1}{2}$ in.*

5. *Two-handled cup. Simon Pantin, 1705. Private Collection.* H. $8\frac{1}{2}$ *in.*

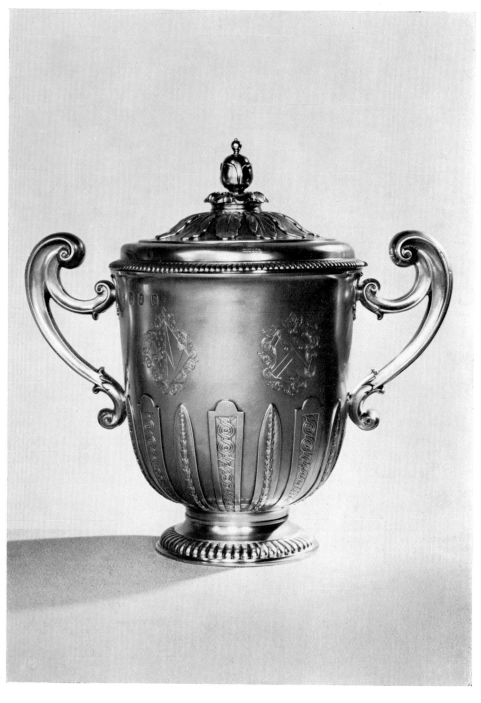

6. *Two-handled cup. Pierre Platel, 1705. Ashmolean Museum. H.* 10½ *in.*

7. *Two-handled cup. David Willaume, 1705. Private Collection.*

8. *Two-handled cup. Paul de Lamerie, 1723. Private Collection.*
*Arms of the Hon. George Treby, M.P. H. 11½ in.*

9. *Two-handled cup. Philip Rollos, 1714. Arms and cipher of George I.*
*From an ambassadorial service.*
*The property of the Marchioness of Cholmondeley. H. 15 in.*

10. *Pair of vases, the cylindrical bodies of carved ivory.*
*David Willaume, 1711. Private Collection. Formerly at Fonthill.*
H. 16¾ *in.*

11. *Flagon, one of a pair. Edward Holaday, 1718. Mercers' Company.*
*H. 18 in.*

12A. *Tankard. Maker's mark VC crowned, 1694.*
*Metropolitan Museum, New York. H. 7¾ in.*
12B. *Tankard. Pierre Harache, 1699.*
*Formerly Fitzhenry Collection.*

13A. *Tankard. Joseph Ward, 1701. Jesus College, Oxford.*
*H. 8½ in.*
13B. *Tankard. John Downes, 1701.*
*Victoria and Albert Museum. H. 6⅞ in.*

14A. *Tankard. Samuel Wastell, 1703.*
*St. Edmund's Hall, Oxford. H. 7¾ in.*
14B. *Tankard. Samuel Margas, 1713. Ironmongers' Company.*
*H. 8⅞ in.*

15A. *Tankard. Mathew Lofthouse, 1713. Oxford Corporation.*
*H. 11 in.*
15B. *Mug. John Boddington, 1698. Messrs. Lumley.*

16A. *Mug, one of a pair. Maker's mark IC with mullet, 1692.*
*Ashmolean Museum. H. 3¾ in.*
16B. *Mug. Maker's mark a goose in a circle, 1693.*
*Ashmolean Museum. H 3¾ in.*

17A. *Covered mug. John Chartier, 1703.*
*Private Collection. H.* $4\frac{3}{4}$ *in.*
17B. *Tumbler from a travelling set.*
*Maker's mark only: TT beneath a coronet.*
*About 1690. Victoria and Albert Museum. H.* $3\frac{1}{4}$ *in.*

18A.  *Monteith with removable rim. Isaac Dighton, 1698.*
*Great Yarmouth Corporation. H.* 13½ *in.*
18B.  *Monteith. Samuel Hood, 1693. Mr. John Wyndham.*
*Diam.* 13⅖ *in.*

19A. *Monteith with removable rim. Edmund Pearse, 1709.*
*Goldsmiths' Company. Diam. 14⅖ in.*
19B. *Punch-bowl. John White, 1726. Jesus College, Oxford. Diam. 19 in.*

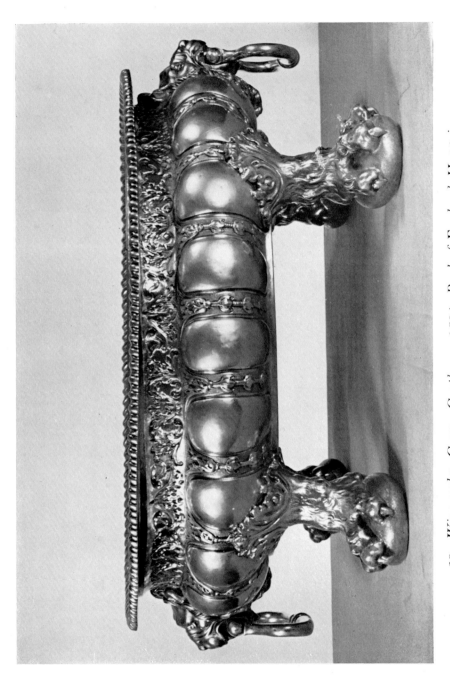

20. *Wine-cooler. George Garthorne, 1694. Bank of England. H. 13 in.*

21. *Wine-cooler. Pierre Harache, 1697. Barber-Surgeons' Company.*
*L. 22 in.*

22. *Wine-cooler. Philip Rollos, 1699.*
*Arms of Evelyn, 5th Earl, afterwards 1st Duke of Kingston.*
*Hermitage Museum, Leningrad. H. 34½ in.*

23. *Wine-cooler. David Willaume, 1708.*
*Crest of George II as Prince of Wales. Duke of Brunswick.*
*From the Cumberland Plate. L. 45 in.*

24. *Wine-cooler. Paul de Lamarie, 1726.*
*Arms of Nicholas, 4th Earl of Scarsdale.*
*Hermitage Museum, Leningrad. H. 35 in.*

25. *Ice pail, one of a pair. Philip Rollos, no date letter. About* 1715–20.
*Arms of John,* 1st *Earl of Bristol. National Trust, Ickworth.*H. 10½ *in.*

26. *Wine fountain. David Willaume, 1701. Duke of Buccleuch.* H. $22\frac{1}{4}$ *in.*

27. *Wine fountain. David Willaume*, 1708. En suite *with No. 23. Duke of Brunswick. From the Cumberland Plate. H.* 42½ *in.*

28. *Wine bottle. George Garthorne, 1690. Arms of George III added later.*
*Royal Plate, Buckingham Palace. H. 17 in.*

29. *Wine bottle. Pierre Harache, 1699. The arms not contemporary. Eton College. H. 21 in.*

30A. *Ewer. Thomas Issod, 1694.*
*Ambassadorial plate with arms of George III added later. Lord Sackville.*
*H. 11¾ in.*

30B. *Jug. William Fawdery, 1722.*
*Christie's. H. 7½ in.*

31.  *Pair of ewers. Pierre Harache, 1697. Earl of Warwick. H. 9⅝ in.*

32. *Jug. Benjamin Pyne, 1699. Magdalen College, Oxford. H. 15 in.*

33. *Jug. Simon Pantin, 1711. Jesus College, Oxford. H. 11½ in.*

34B. *Ewer. David Willaume, 1700.*
*Victoria and Albert Museum. H. 8¼ in.*

34A. *Ewer. Pierre Harache, 1697.*
*The arms not contemporary. Vintners' Company. H. 10½ in.*

35B. *Ewer. Edward Vincent, 1713.
Trinity College, Oxford. H. 14⅝ in.*

35A. *Ewer. Pierre Platel, 1714.
Victoria and Albert Museum. H. 9 in.*

36B. *Shaving jug. Anne Tanqueray, 1729.*
*Arms of Lionel, 4th Earl of Dysart. Christie's.*
*H. 8 in.*

36A. *Shaving dish. Francis Garthorne, 1689.*
*Arms and cipher of William III. Christie's. Diam. $12\frac{3}{4}$ in.*

37. *Punch-bowl. John Le Sage, 1725. Arms of Henry, 3rd Baron Barnard. The property of the Marchioness of Cholmondeley. H. 9 in.*

38. *Toilet service of 32 pieces. Benjamin Pyne, 1708. Arms of Howard, Dukes of Norfolk. Christie's.*

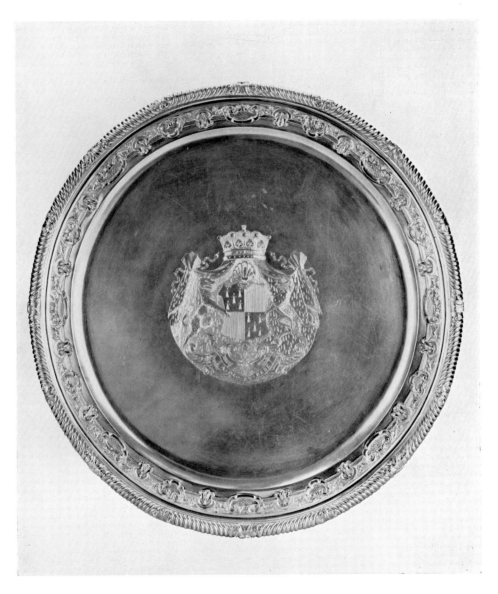

39. *Salver. John Le Sage, 1727.*
*Arms of Philip, 4th Earl of Chesterfield.*
*Victoria and Albert Museum. Diam.* 14¾ *in.*

40A. *Teapot and stand. Simon Pantin, 1705.*
*Victoria and Albert Museum. H. 8½ in.*
40B. *Teapot and stand. Louis Cuny, 1710. Messrs. Lumley.*

41A. *Teapot. James Seabrook,* 1718. *Ashmolean Museum.*
*H. 5¾ in.*
41B. *Teapot. Jacob Margas,* 1719.
*Assheton Bennett Collection. H. 5 in.*

42. *Teapot. David Willaume, 1706. Assheton Bennett Collection.*
H. $6\frac{7}{8}$ *in.*

43. *Tea-kettle and stand. Samuel Margas, 1715. Private Collection.*
*H. 15 in.*

44A. *Teapot and stand. Anthony Nelme, 1708.*
*Assheton Bennett Collection. H. 7½ in.*
44B. *Teapot. James Smith, 1719. Victoria and Albert Museum.*
*H. 4 in.*

45A. *Pair of teacups and saucer stands.*
*Maker's mark FS with crown above and mullet below*, 1688.
*Private Collection. Diam. of cup 3 in., diam. of saucer 5⅛ in.*
45B. *Teacup and saucer. Unmarked, early eighteenth century.*
*Victoria and Albert Museum.*
*H. of cup 1⅞ in., diam. of saucer 4 in.*

46B. *Tea-caddy. John Farnell, 1717. Victoria and Albert Museum. H. 5 in.*

46A. *Tea-caddy. Isaac Liger(?), early eighteenth century. Engraved with designs after Simon Gribelin. C. D. Rotch Collection. H. 4⅜ in.*

47. *Pair of saucers with trembleuse stands. David Tanqueray, 1718. Private Collection. Diam. of saucer $5\frac{1}{4}$ in.*

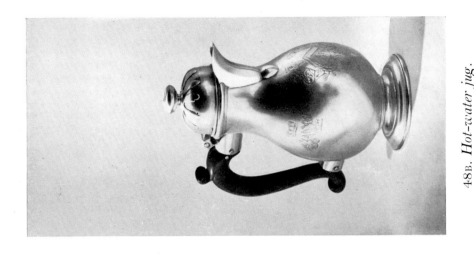

48B. Hot-water jug.
Simon Pantin, 1712.
Assheton Bennett Collection.
H. 6½ in.

48A. Milk jug. Thomas Folkingham, 1712.
Messrs Lumley.

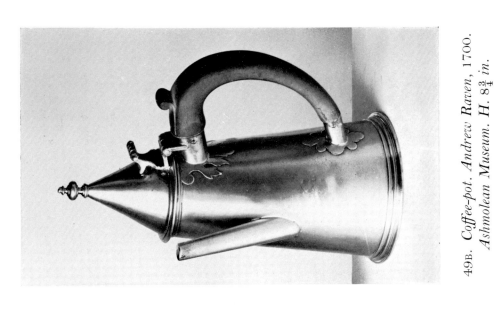

49B. *Coffee-pot. Andrew Raven, 1700.
Ashmolean Museum. H. 8¾ in.*

49A. *Coffee-pot. George Garthorne, 1690.
Assheton Bennett Collection.
H. 9⅜ in.*

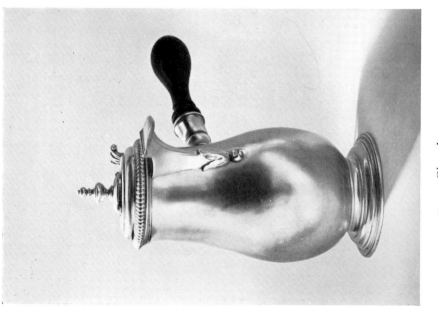

50A. *Chocolate-pot.*
*Pierre Platel, 1705.*
*Assheton Bennett Collection. H. 9 in.*

50B. *Chocolate-pot. Thomas Corbet, 1703. Christie's.*
*H. 11 in.*

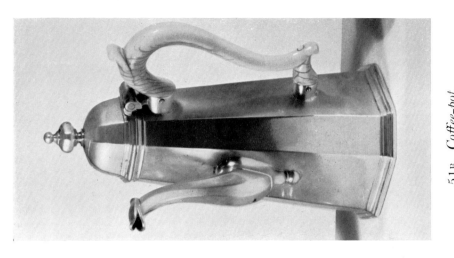

51B. *Coffee-pot.*
*Anthony Nelme, 1720.*
*Christie's. H. 9¼ in.*

51A. *Coffee-pot. Humphrey Payne, 1703.*
*Assheton Bennett Collection.*
*H. 10¼ in.*

52A. *Chocolate-pot.*
*William Fawdery, 1704.*
*Victoria and Albert Museum. H.* 10¾ *in.*
52B. *Coffee-pot.*
*Maker's mark only:*
*BB with crown above and mullet below.*
*About 1715. Christie's. H.* 11¼ *in.*

53. *Coffee-pot and stand. Samuel Wastell, 1702. Private Collection.*

54A. *Hot-water jug.*
*Anthony Nelme, 1713.*
*Ashmolean Museum. H. 5¾ in.*
54B. *Hot-water jug.*
*Jonathan Madden, 1702.*
*Ashmolean Museum. H. 5½ ins.*

55A. *Hot-water jug. Philip Rollos, 1710.*
*Arms and cipher of Queen Anne.*
*Lord Sackville. H. 7½ in.*
55B. *Hot-water jug. Thomas Parr, 1709.*
*Assheton Bennett Collection. H. 6⅞ in.*

56A. *Sugar bowl.*
*Francis Garthorne, 1691.*
*Assheton Bennett Collection.* H. $5\frac{1}{2}$ *in.*
56B. *Sugar bowl.*
*Samuel Wastell, 1713.*
*Assheton Bennett Collection.* H. $4\frac{7}{8}$ *in.*

57A. *Sugar bowl.*
*William Fleming, 1718.*
*Assheton Bennett Collection. H. 3 in.*
57B. *Sugar bowl.*
*Robert Lucas, 1728.*
*Assheton Bennett Collection. H. 3 in.*

58A. *Sugar bowl. Pierre Harache, 1704. Messrs. Lumley. Diam.* $6\frac{1}{4}$ *in.*
58B. *Bread basket. Thomas Folkingham, 1711.*
*The arms not contemporary. Victoria and Albert Museum.* H. $5\frac{3}{8}$ *in.*

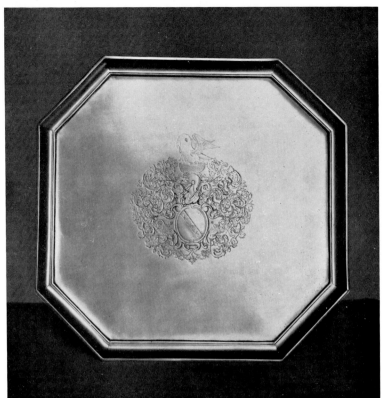

59A. *Tray. Pierre Platel, 1710. Christie's. W. 18¼ in.*
59B. *Tray. Francis Nelme, 1725. Christie's. Diam. 10¼ in.*

60. *Plate. Francis Garthorne, 1690. Crowned cipher of William and Mary. Private Collection. Diam.* $9\frac{3}{8}$ *in.*

61. *Dish, one of a pair. Benjamin Pyne, 1698.*
*Arms of Sir William Courtenay of Powderham Castle.*
*Victoria and Albert Museum. W. 9½ in.*

62. *Basin. Paul de Lamerie, 1723. Private Collection. Diam. 24 in.*

63. *Detail of cast and chiselled escutcheon with the arms of the Hon. George Treby, M.P., from the basin on Pl. 62.*

64. *Basin. Paul de Lamerie, 1722. Ashmolean Museum. Diam.* 21½ *in.*

65A. *Tureen. Maker's mark only: Simon Pantin. About* 1726.
*From a service ordered in London for the Empress Catherine of Russia.*
*Hermitage Museum, Leningrad. H.* 11½ *in.*
65B. *Sauce-boat. Benjamin Pyne,* 1723. *Crest of Howard, Dukes of Norfolk.*
*Christie's. W.* 9 *in.*

66A. *Salt cellar. Maker's mark ET with two pellets*, 1695.
*Victoria and Albert Museum. H.* 2½ *in.*
66B. *Salt cellar. Matthew Cooper*, 1707.
*Victoria and Albert Museum. H.* 1½ *in.*

67A. *Salt cellar, one of a pair. Thomas Folkingham, 1714.*
*Metropolitan Museum. W. 3 in.*
67B. *Salt cellar, one of a pair. Anne Tanqueray, 1726.*
*Victoria and Albert Museum. H. 3½ in.*

68A. *Salt cellar. Louis Cuny, 1697. Upholders' Company.* H. $4\frac{5}{8}$ *in.*
68B. *Box salt cellar. David Tanqueray, 1715. Private Collection.*
H. $2\frac{1}{2}$ *in.*

69A. *Écuelle. Pierre Platel, 1704. Private Collection. Diam.* $6\frac{7}{8}$ *in.*
69B. *Écuelle. Isaac Liger, 1726. Ashmolean Museum. W.* $10\frac{5}{8}$ *in.*

70A. *Porringer. William Keatt, 1698. Victoria and Albert Museum.*
*Diam.* $5\frac{1}{4}$ *in.*
70B. *Chamber candlestick. Louis Cuny, 1703. Private Collection. H. 2 in.*

71A. *Wall-sconce.*
*John Barnard, 1699.*
*Bank of England. H. 11¾ in*
71B. *Wall-sconce.*
*John Fawdery, 1702.*
*Christie's H. 9½ in.*

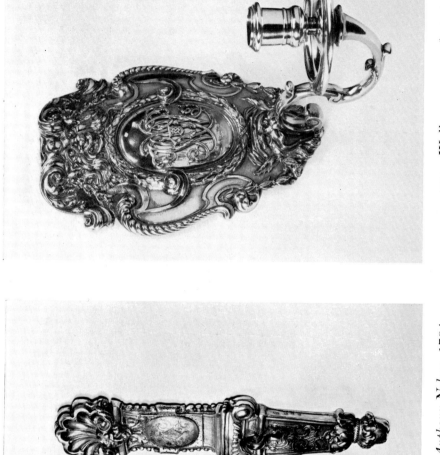

72B. *Wall-sconce, one of a pair.*
*Isaac Liger, 1709. Christie's. H. 8 in.*

72A. *Wall-sconce. Anthony Nelme, 1704.*
*Arms of Frances, widow of Christopher,*
*2nd Viscount Castlecomer.*
*Christie's. H. 13¾ in.*

73c. *Candlestick, one of a pair.*
*W. Denny and John Backe, 1698.*
*Christie's. H. 7½ in.*

73b. *Candlestick, one of a set of four,*
*and a snuffer-stand.*
*Joseph Bird, 1700.*
*Ashmolean Museum. H. 9¼ in.*

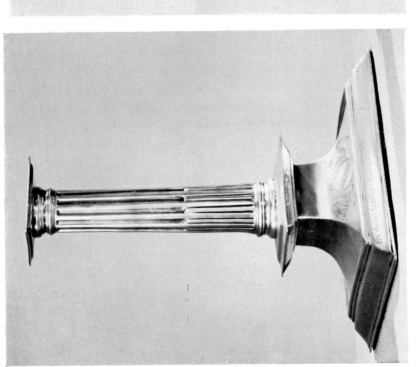

73a. *Candlestick, one of a set of six.*
*Maker's mark WE a mullet above and below, 1692.*
*Middle Temple. H. 12 in.*

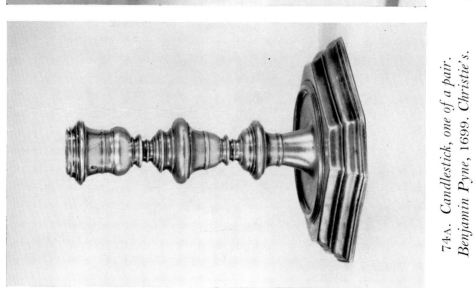

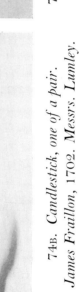

74C. *Candlestick. David Green, 1720.*
*Victoria and Albert Museum.*
H. 6¾ in.

74B. *Candlestick, one of a pair.*
*James Fraillon, 1702. Messrs. Lumley.*

74A. *Candlestick, one of a pair.*
*Benjamin Pyne, 1699. Christie's.*
H. 7½ in.

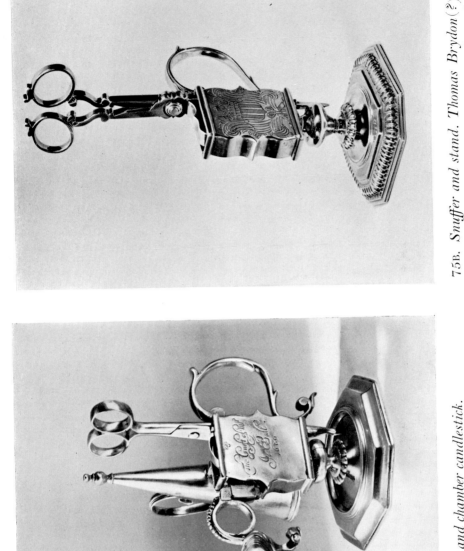

75B. *Snuffer and stand. Thomas Brydon(?), 1696.*
*Victoria and Albert Museum. H. of stand* $4\frac{1}{4}$ *in.*

75A. *Snuffer and chamber candlestick.*
*Maker's mark W B mullet below, 1688.*
*Assheton Bennett Collection. H.* $6\frac{3}{4}$ *in.*

76A. *Snuffer and stand. Anthony Blackford, 1704.*
*Assheton Bennett Collection. H. 8 in.*
76B. *Snuffer and stand. Thomas Brydon, 1697.*
*Assheton Bennett Collection. H. 7⅛ in.*

77. *Chandelier. Maker's mark only: George Garthorne. About* 1690.
*Hampton Court Palace.*

78A. *Set of three casters. John Edwards, 1701. The arms not contemporary.*
*John Wyndham Esq. H. 10 in. and 7⅜ in.*
78B. (centre) *Caster. John Chartier, 1699. Christie's. H. 8½ in.*
(left and right) *Two from a set of three casters.*
*Benjamin Blakeley, 1718. Christie's. H. 7¼ in.*

79A. *Set of three casters, one with blind piercing for use as a mustard-pot.*
*Maker's mark only: George Garthorne. About 1700.*
*Contemporary arms of John Methuen, ambassador to Portugal.*
*Christie's. H. 9½ in. and 7¾ in.*
79B. *Set of three casters. Simon Pantin, 1716.*
*Victoria and Albert Museum. H. 8¼ in. and 6 in.*

80A. *Cruet and stand. Maker's mark only: George Garthorne.*
*About* 1700. *Private Collection.*
80B. *Cruet and stand. Paul de Lamerie,* 1727. *Ashmolean Museum.*
*H.* 8 *in.*

81A. *Dredger. No maker's mark*, 1720.
*Victoria and Albert Museum. H.* $3\frac{1}{2}$ *in.*
81B. *Inkstand. Anthony Nelme*, 1717.
*Assheton Bennett Collection. H.* $3\frac{1}{4}$ *in.*

82A. *Inkstand. James Fraillon, 1716. Arms and cipher of George I.*
*Royal Plate, Windsor Castle. L. 11 in.*
82B. *Inkstand. David Willaume, Jr., 1727.*
*Arms of Tollemache impaling Carteret for Lionel, 4th Earl of Dysart.*
*Christie's. L. 13 in.*

83. *Tobacco boxes. Assheton Bennett Collection.*

A. *Matthew Pickering, 1705. L. 3⅝ in.*
B. *Robert Cooper, 1688. L. 3⅝ in.*

C. *Edward Cornock, 1710. L. 3⅝ in.*
D. *Maker's mark SH a rosette below, 1685. L. 3⅝ in.*

84. *Detail of top of table* (Pl. 85A), *engraved with the royal arms and badges of William and Mary. Signed:* 'R.H.SCAP'. *Royal Plate, Windsor Castle.*

85B. *Andiron, one of a pair.*
*Andrew Moore, 1696. Cipher of William III.*
*Royal Plate, Buckingham Palace. H. 17 in.*

85A. *Side view of silver table presented to William III by the*
*Corporation of London. Andrew Moore, no date letter.*
*About 1690. H. 2 ft. 9½ in. W. 4 ft.*

86. *Silver mirror frame*, en suite *with the table on* Pl. 85A.
*Andrew Moore, no date letter. About* 1690.
*Arms and crowned cipher of William and Mary.*
*Royal Plate, Windsor Castle. H.* 7 *ft.* 6 *in.*

87. *Silver throne and footstool. Nicholas Clausen, 1713.*
*Made for Peter the Great, Emperor of Russia.*
*Hermitage Museum, Leningrad. H. 5 ft. 10 in.*

88. *Dish. Pierre Harache, 1695. The engraving attributed to Simon Gribelin. Formerly in the Swaythling Collection. W. 16 in.*

89A. Page from Benjamin Rhodes' A New Book of Cyphers, London, 1723. British Museum.

89B. Page from Benjamin Rhodes' account book with a counterproof of his engraving of the arms of the Duke of St. Albans. Hoare's Bank.

90. *Title-page of Simon Gribelin's second* Book of Ornaments, 1700.
*British Museum.*

91A. *Title-page of Simon Gribelin's first Book of Ornaments, 1697.*
*British Museum.*

91B. *Proof from a silver salver engraved by Simon Gribelin for Henry Boyle, Chancellor of the Irish Exchequer, on the death of William III in 1702. From Gribelin's album.*
*British Museum.*

92. *Salver. Marks obliterated. About* 1695. *Engraved by Simon Gribelin for Charles, afterwards* 3rd *Earl of Halifax, with the Exchequer seal of William and Mary. Burrell Collection, Glasgow Museum. Diam.* 13½ *in.*

93. *Salver. William Lukin,* 1717. *Arms of Richard, 5th Viscount Ingram, impaling those of his wife, Lady Anne Howard. The engraving signed by Joseph Simpson. Victoria and Albert Museum. Diam.* 14½ *in.*

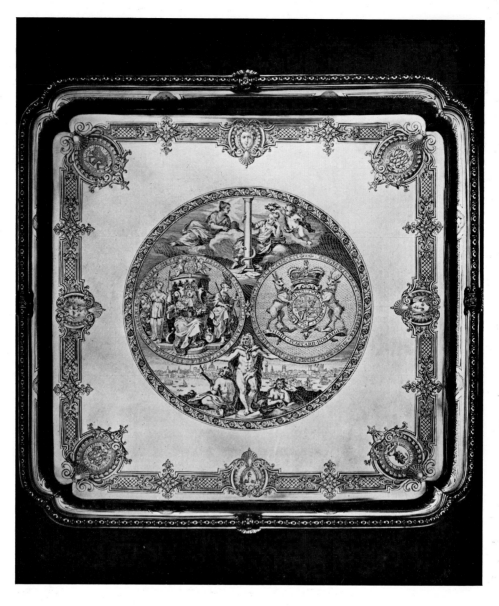

94. *Salver. Paul de Lamerie, 1727.*
*Made from the second Exchequer seal of George I for Sir Robert Walpole.*
*The engraving attributed to William Hogarth.*
*Victoria and Albert Museum. W.* 19¼ *in.*

95. *Trade-card of Ellis Gamble, Goldsmith, engraved by William Hogarth. About 1716. British Museum.*

96. *Proof from a salver engraved with a scene from the* Rape of the Lock.
*Signed by* William Hogarth *and dated* 1716 (*printed in reverse*).
*British Museum.*